CULTURAL CANCER

Treating
the Disease
of Political Correctness

Daryl Kane

2017

Arjuna's Arrow Publishing

CULTURAL CANCER

Treating the Disease of Political Correctness

Address inquiries to arjunasarrow.com or darylkane23@gmail.com.

Available at Amazon.com and other online outlets.

Second Edition

ISBN-13: 978-0692939178
ISBN-10: 0692939172

Dedicated to my father

Contents

Preface to the 2nd Edition   1

Foreword   11

1   The Great Conflict   16

2   What is Political Correctness?   19

3   Where Does Political Correctness Come From?   22

4   Political Correctness in Academia   25

5   Political Correctness in Popular Culture   36

6   The Democratic Party Makes a Deal With the Devil   52

7   The Silent Revolution   57

8   What Now?   63

9   Political Correctness as Mental Illness   66

10   Attacking Political Correctness as a Private Citizen   70

11   Social Media Batman   82

12   Attacking Political Correctness as a Media Creator   88

13   Battling Political Correctness as a Politician   95

14   Conclusion   110

Epilogue   112

About the Author   124

Preface to the 2nd Edition

The first edition of this book was largely an unpolished work that was rushed in order to time-stamp particularly important concepts that had been ignored for decades and were suddenly beginning to punch through. These important, previously suppressed viewpoints run counter to patently false narratives that have been force-fed to two generations of Americans. Until very recently, pushback on things like victim-feminism and false assertions of racial biases were not only off-limits in the secular progressive circles that relentlessly pushed them, but also to those in the so-called conservative circles who lacked the courage to oppose them. All too often we saw, and continue to see, conservatives who dare speak up to challenge any of the Left's sacred cows, such as gender identity or racial demagoguery, immediately sold out by the "good" members of their caucus.

This phenomenon persists to this day, and while Republican establishment pushback remains timid at best, there is now a very real grassroots movement which openly mocks political correctness, gleefully poking holes in the massive hot-air balloon. The general political thesis of this book and the outline provided for reclaiming our countries and culture has very much in common with what has come to be known as "populist nationalism." At a time when conservative think tanks were calling for a surrender on social issues and an increased focus on economic conservativism, this book, and the populist nationalism movement, calls for the opposite. This fundamental distinction is borne from the simple fact that the Left has chosen to lead with social issues and wait for everything else to follow. By surrendering on social issues we play directly into their hands. This is no doubt the reason why this is the path our enemies constantly encourage us to take. The Left's vision of our political future is a country where the insane "progressive" views on social issues become the shared, core common beliefs of the electorate, and a thoroughly neutered conservative movement led by people like Gary Johnson is permitted to chime in on occasion to push back on marginal tax increases. That Gary Johnson was chosen to lead the Libertarian Party, historically to the right of the Republican Party, demonstrates the Left's success in recalibrating our political landscape.

But we have also seen a President elected by tapping into this grassroots movement—ergo the addition of a hopeful

Epilogue in this edition. As the first printing and the ideas behind it pre-date this movement it should be read neither as an endorsement or a rejection of the Donald Trump phenomenon. Excluding the Epilogue, which was written following the 2016 Presidential election, nothing has been reworked to incorporate or address this remarkable event (though certain chapters have been updated, such as the inclusion of the segment on Colin Kaepernick in chapter 5, written at the outset of his tawdry protest before it metastasized throughout the NFL the following season). There is a genuine desire by both the Left as well as the Trump ever-faithful to put everyone and everything into a "pro-Trump" or "anti-Trump" box to suit their own interests. By pre-dating the Trump era this book maintains its own separate identity from this new binary reality. It is left to the reader to draw any conclusions from the ideas expressed herein relative to "Trumpism." All that I as author will state is that these plainly clear and obvious ideas, previously obscured through clever manipulation, have existed for quite some time and were ripe for the taking. Trump certainly capitalized on some though not all of these ideas—ideas and straight talk which are so powerful that just the occasional hint of them, combined with the right personality and the strike of lightning, were able to catch fire and ride all the way into the White House. Whether or not Trump is willing or able to govern with these ideas remains to be seen. The distinction here being that the ideas existed before Trump and thus manifested through him, but not from him.

It is the hope of those of us who have been pushing back all the while against political correctness in our personal spheres of influence, that he will use the bully pulpit to make good on the promise of his presidency. We will carry on the work with or without him. President Trump represents a double-edged sword for those seeking a definitive rejection of political correctness. It's true that where previously there was little or no hope to be found, a light can now be seen at the end of a very long tunnel. The degree to which Trump is cognizant of the larger issues at work remains to be seen, but it is important to recognize that the Left also sees an opportunity with Trump. In his tendency to speak off the cuff—often effectively but other times to his detriment—and his propensity for unforced errors, they see a potential reboot of the disgracing of Richard Nixon. That epochal event, the earliest and perhaps still greatest victory of the Left, laid the groundwork for their 50-year assault on

American values, otherwise known as the Culture War. Should they succeed in tearing down the Trump administration they hope to similarly dispatch any of the important ideas outlined in books such as this one by attaching them to him, and permanently snuff out this most timid repudiation of the politically correct insanity that has just begun to emerge. My suggestion is to broadly support this administration, fervently when it stands up for our interests, but to also retain a healthy degree of objectivity, intellectual vigilance and your own ideologically independent identity. Should the Left succeed in ousting Trump they will no doubt attempt to cast out all of the good conservative voices who have emerged in recent years along with the many anti-PC "Breitbart" style news outlets.

Whereas it's important to protect the identity of our ideas from individual politicians it's also important to prevent allowing our movement to be lumped into categories or labels. Since this book was first written we've also seen the emergence of what has come to be known as the "alt-right," which takes credit for much of what has occurred. Many of the ideas espoused in this work could easily be regarded as fitting within the alt-right framework, and the alt-right deserves credit for being the first named movement to take on the politically correct narratives in a meaningful way. But it is also true that within the fringes of this movement there exist things which must remain unacceptable, such as anti-Semitism and other forms of racism. While the cultural and political persecution of whites is a central component of what we are up against, any reclamation of white European dignity in its host nations must begin with the fundamental reclamation of the same rights to organize and speak freely that are encouraged and afforded to every other group ("multiculturalism"). Any efforts to do so will be met with chargers of "racism," a dynamic that must be overcome if whites have any hope of surviving their political genocide. Shattering these deeply entrenched cultural narratives requires both courage and discipline; and while subversive commentary is necessary, the last thing that is needed is for those in our ranks to engage in or espouse ideas that directly reinforce the false narratives we are seeking to dismantle. Whites standing up for themselves are no more or less racist than blacks, Hispanics or Muslims organizing around their interests, unless we in fact march alongside neo-Nazis and white supremacists. The truth is our greatest weapon, and any progress achieved by an organization advocating white interests would be outweighed by the harm done by such groups, and be immediately exploited by the Left. And so while the alt-right made positive contributions to the political landscape, if they do in fact turn out to be poisoned by Nazism, we must be prepared and capable of moving our ideas, purity intact, to a new ideological location.

But let us hope that the Trump administration *will* succeed and lead to many others like it, both here at home and overseas with our European friends, with whom the situation is substantially more dire. Over here, traditional white European Americans look to be supplanted in two or three generations by a myriad of immigrants actively recruited to vote against them—but who actually share many of our Judeo-Christian values and thus could end up proving to be political allies. Open borders in Europe, however, has led to a massive influx of predominantly Islamic immigrants from the Middle East and Africa who are openly encouraged by their religious leaders to march through the back door and take over—to use Europe's democracy and freedom to destroy its democracy and freedom.

The invasion of Europe by Muslims has happened before. Where in the past these conquests were military, the current invasion is achieved by political inertia—and eventually, surrender. As European elites equate Trump to Hitler for calling for a more thorough examination of peoples emigrating from historically hostile Middle Eastern countries, Islamic imams are encouraging Muslims to take the low hanging fruit, Europe, by simply moving there and having as many children as possible while ensuring their progeny resist the contamination of Western values.

Political correctness has changed society's organizing principle from that which mutually benefits all to one revolving around female empowerment. This, among other things, has led to alarmingly low birth rates that, combined with lax immigration policies, make Europe ripe for the taking for any God-fearing people with patriarchal values willing to simply relocate and multiply. It is both ironic and alarming that those taking advantage of these aggressively leftist policies are quite possibly the least socially tolerant people on the planet.

I'm not saying that Muslims are inherently bad people who should not be allowed into Western countries. As this book repeatedly posits, all individuals regardless of race or creed emerge in this world with just as much potential to contribute positively or negatively to their world. But immigration must never be allowed to alter or threaten the cultural identity of a nation-state. Due to a variety of concerning viewpoints within the Koran that appear to clash with the basic foundational concepts of Western Civilization, a sober and clear-minded evaluation of anyone adhering to those beliefs must be conducted before permitting them into our country. The longer we allow these societal transformations to continue the fewer and less pleasant the available remedies become.

As Donald Trump successfully tapped into the ideas contained herein, so too can Americans in a variety of sectors cash in on them. In an age where late-night television is comprised of talentless, SJW hacks masquerading as comedians there need be only one brave pioneer willing to wade into a different source for material to start a trend that will force the progressive producers to make tough decisions. It won't be easy and it won't happen overnight, but if we persist the cultural elites will eventually understand that if they wish to continue to profit from their endeavors they must choose between either offering a fresh (revolutionary to them) perspective or continuing to hammer home a tired one and losing their audience to their competitors. Culturally and politically the only choice is political correctness or its rejection. The advantages of the former are many: substantially easier access to platforms, endless high-fives from friends, and aggressive shouting down of anyone who doesn't enjoy your work. The advantages of the latter is that you are offering something new over something stale, and that while developing your work you are looking for things that are real rather than chasing illusions. In the end, the lesson of Donald Trump, that the truth remains as it has always been and always will be, is an incredibly powerful one. And in a climate where truth is being outlawed, even the faintest drop of it can quite literally change the world.

# # #

Foreword

Earlier this year droves of progressives stood up and applauded as Bruce Jenner heroically embraced her "true" identity as Caitlyn. A week later however, the same do-gooders find themselves doing a bit of soul searching as they feel inexplicably ambivalent towards Rachel Dolezal. If they accept the notion that gender is a social construct, an illusion, why don't they feel the same way about ethnicity? Are they, too, guilty of prejudice? In their efforts to abolish the constant barrage of bigotry that is Western Civilization, had they neglected to fully purify themselves? For those of you asking yourselves this question, don't worry. Remove the belt from around your neck and slowly step down from the chair. Take a deep breath and repeat after me: It's not your fault. It's not your fault.

The reason why you felt compelled to cheer for Jenner but not Rachel Dolezal is actually quite simple. It's because you hadn't been told to yet.

When Rachel Dolezal began her transracial journey she made one tragic mistake. She didn't allow the Left to tell everyone how heroic she was first. You see, "Caitlyn" Jenner had the luxury of emerging on stage after Americans had already been thoroughly "educated" about the wonders of transgenderism. Their professors at P.C. University had already enlightened college students about the age-old historical struggle between a community created a few decades ago and the forces of reactionary, patriarchal evil. This lesson had been reinforced by the charming depictions of the transgendered hero that graced our televisions and the snide put-downs of anyone who dared oppose their struggle for liberation. And ultimately, even if you lived under a rock or managed to navigate around your college indoctrination, activist judges made it clear. Transgenderism and the surgical mutilation of one's reproductive organs is not only perfectly normal, it's actually quite heroic. Besides, isn't it covered under Obamacare?

For those of you still with me the lesson is clear. Don't wait for the loony Left to tell another generation what is and is not "normal." The antidote to the absurdity of political correctness is a hearty dose of common sense. The Left is fully aware of this fact which is why they've put so much effort into bullying us away from debating cultural issues. Meanwhile, as we timidly retreat, the Left defines the rules and boundaries of the conversation in such a manner that by the time it starts we have already been disqualified. Those of us who still rely on rational thought must not only make our voices heard during the debate but must also insist on having a say in defining the narrative.

The Left will argue that parallels between Jenner and Dolezal are faulty because Jenner announced his/her "trans" identity openly, while Dolezal appears to be using it as a defense after being caught in lie. This is not altogether untrue, but even if this narrative survives they will not be able to avoid answering the simple question: Does transethnicity exist? As is often the case with politically correct assertions, there is no answer to that question that doesn't lead to a paradox. If the answer is Yes, and if ethnicity truly is yet another "social construct," why are campuses so obsessed with determining the ethnicity of their applicants? If the answer is No, how can you accept the notion of transgenderism when society began its horrific habit of classifying its members as male or female long before it began classifying them as black or white?

Traditionally the Left's response to the numerous paradoxes created by politically correct orthodoxy has been silence. That is to say, they have relied on their unilateral control over the portals of public discourse (mainstream media, academia, the entertainment industry, etc.) to swiftly eliminate any such questioning before anyone gets a chance to even think about it.

The purveyors of political correctness have created a strange world where things like gender and ethnicity are fluid or imagined and the only constants are racism, sexism and white-male privilege. It's a world where the deranged are given free rein to project their delusions on the masses and those that don't pretend to see it are the ones diagnosed with phobias. They've had a great deal of success growing this world, so much so that a majority of Americans twice elected a proud proponent of it. But there is one fatal flaw in the design of their world. It is built on ideas and premises that have no basis in reality and are diametrically opposed to natural law, logic and reason. That's why a seemingly minor and trivial story like Rachel Dolezal can prove to be so powerful—because political correctness is a bubble of hot air that depends upon a massive defense apparatus for survival. A massive, taxpayer funded machine that aims to pulverize any and all obstacles, be it a politician, business or private citizen. For the most part the Left has done an impeccable job protecting the masses from dissenting views and free speech, but inevitably something was bound to slip through.

Rachel Dolezal not only happened, America knows it happened, and for the first time in a long time they are seeing political correctness for exactly what it is: a whole lot of nonsense.

# # #

1

The Great Conflict

For the past several hundred years American politics have been viewed within the context of a two-party system. Republicans and Democrats have evolved their positions relative to the electorate over time and occasionally switched positions. The two-party struggle is very much relevant here in the 21st century but it is now an ancillary conflict, secondary to an ultimate war being waged all across Western Civilization between the forces of cultural patriotism and cultural terrorism. The cultural terrorism referred to is the bizarre ideological phenomenon known as political correctness. This truth is not wholly distinct from the two-party struggle (in fact as we will discuss later, they are closely related) but it is important to recognize that the two-party system has adapted to address the phenomenon of political correctness and not vice-versa. Thus, the anti-American values of political correctness existed before they became accepted as orthodoxy for the Democratic Party. A conscious decision was made to partner with a treasonous movement for political expediency. The

Republican Party's response (or lack thereof) has been one of confused bewilderment. They have been frequently tricked into digging their own graves by perpetuating the numerous falsehoods of political correctness. The Republican Party has proven to be weak, clumsy and largely blind to the crux of a fifty-year culture war with an enemy whose tactics they still fail to grasp.

The unilateral failures of the Republican Party are undeniable and they bear considerable blame for the shocking nature of what has occurred in America. Nevertheless, they have become the de facto party for patriots due to the fact that they are not the aggressors. They are not the party that bought electoral stock in a declining America. They are merely the party that did nothing meaningful to prevent its spread. As such, the indictment of the Democratic Party becomes the singular endorsement for the Republican Party.

Before proceeding any further I feel the need to emphasize that while the bomb of political correctness was first set off in the United States, the epidemic has spread across all of Western Civilization and much of the rest of the world. As such, the contents of this book can be understood and implemented in most Western countries by substituting the Republican and Democratic parties with your local conservative or progressive parties and movements. The purpose of this work is to help spread awareness about the nature of the enemy while presenting a practical blueprint for resistance to be used by private citizens and elected officials alike.

# # #

2

What is Political Correctness?

It's hard to fight something you don't understand, so let's start by dissecting political correctness beginning with a simple question: What exactly *is* political correctness? If you ask the average, reasonably-informed citizen to define it, most would describe it as a mindset of hyper-sensitivity to the feelings of others, particularly regarding ethnicity, gender, religion, or sexual orientation. This assessment has some truth to it, but it misses a very big point.

Let's look at religion as an example. Political correctness informs us that we must be sensitive to Islam and its relationship to terrorism. This courtesy, however, is not extended to Christianity. Political correctness comes to the defense of Islam when its followers commit terrible atrocities, but it searches for opportunities to condemn Christians as bigots. This bizarre contradiction is odd, but far from unique. Across the board, when one looks at the various ways in which people can be categorized, we can draw a clear distinction between groups promoted by PC values and those demonized by them.

The common denominator among groups benefiting from political correctness is that they are not traditionally associated with American power. Be it women in the workplace, minorities from non-European countries applying to colleges, or people engaging in alternative sexual lifestyles, political correctness expands the influence and collective voice of these groups. Political correctness is a forced choosing of that which is alien or new to America over that which is traditional. This is not to say, as Jerry Seinfeld would say, that there is anything wrong with these groups. It is merely an acknowledgement that political correctness actively discriminates against what is traditionally perceived as "American."

Political correctness fails the laugh test when confronted by its own absurdity. But the laughter quickly fades when one contemplates the degree to which Western life is influenced by political correctness. Not only is PC sensibility promoted at all levels of popular culture, but it has taken unilateral control of public education. So much so that one could easily argue education's primary focus has shifted from teaching the three Rs to ideological indoctrination. So much so that Jerry Seinfeld will no longer perform on college campuses.

Identity politics is not the only issue covered by political correctness. Political correctness also speaks to foreign policy and national security. Whether the issue is ISIS or having secure national borders, the American liberal can usually be found defending our enemies and those seeking to undermine America. At the very least, they occupy the part of the discussion least interested in defending America.

For this reason, political correctness as a collective force represents the single greatest threat to America, because it simultaneously coalesces around and amplifies all of the threats that we face. There is a name for political movements that spread their ideas by converting public institutions into political weapons: "fascism." When it is not politically correct for a nation to treat fairly the peoples that built it, or to defend itself from outside threats, it becomes imperative that citizens begin to seriously question the politics of the day.

# # #

21

3

Where Does Political Correctness Come From?

Political Correctness is the weaponized version of what is known as Cultural Marxism. Marxist theory stated that when war came to Europe it would be a war of class rather than country. World War I proved that theory wrong. The communist revolution came to Russia but it failed to impact the rest of Europe. Uprisings were attempted in other countries but the working class people did not behave as the theorists predicted and their leaders were isolated and destroyed. The revolution hadn't spread, it had stalled. But the Marxists weren't prepared to concede their theory to history. Instead, they attempted to learn from the failure and adapt their tactics.

The Marxists ultimately concluded that the reason the workers had not risen up in unison across Europe was because they were blinded by their religious and national identities. Before the workers could recognize their true oppressors they would first need to be liberated from their cultural identity. In 1923 a wealthy communist named Felix Weil used his resources to summon the greatest Marxist thinkers to Germany where they began working in a concerted effort to perfect the formula for revolution. Ultimately, the Frankfurt School was established to provide a base of operations for the ideological warfare the communists were planning. By 1930 their viewpoints and strategies had evolved to such a degree that the Russian communists refuse to endorse their work.

The crux of what emerged from the Frankfurt School was a strategy that emphasized *cultural* Marxism first, *economic* secondary. They created "deconstructionism" and "critical theory" which are two schools of thought that do exactly what you'd imagine. They criticize and deconstruct every aspect of a society from its religion, its ethnicities and even the roles gender play within families. Sound familiar yet? Shortly thereafter Hitler and the Nazis came to power and the primarily Jewish group of thinkers was forced to flee Germany. They were given safe haven in America and reestablished their work inside Columbia University. The revelation that the point of entry for Cultural Marxism into American life was academia should come as no surprise to anyone who has set foot on a college campus in the last 40 years. Many of the movement's leaders would eventually make their way into Hollywood as well, creating a powerful two-pronged weapon to be used against America.

# # #

4

Political Correctness in Academia

There's a classic scene in *Jurassic Park* where the park's banner falls over the T-Rex as he roars into the main lobby. It's certainly not the subtlest of visual puns but it's a powerful one nonetheless, and the image has since become an icon for the flawed hubris of man.

Today a similar scene is unfolding before the eyes of the public on college campuses across the country. The monster behind the current carnage is a group of academic elites who have instituted a bizarre form of politically correct fascism that comes equipped with a massive brainwashing apparatus as well as a rather large stick for silencing dissent. The installation of this apparatus isn't news to anyone who has set foot on a college campus in the last several decades. What *is* news is that this story is finally being reported, at least by any news sources not completely in the tank for the anti-American zealots otherwise known as "social justice warriors." But even those weaponized news sources are now being forced to report on what is happening, even if their slant is predictably 180 degrees out of phase with reality. On this both sides can agree: something is happening.

As previously explained, after the communist revolution stalled in Europe after World War I, the Marxists sought to regroup in Germany and established a massive think tank called The Frankfurt School. The general thrust of what emerged from their discourse was that the reason why the revolution failed to manifest across Europe was because the emphasis had been placed on economic issues rather than cultural ones. Only after dismantling a people's ethnic, religious and national identities could they be made to accept communist ideology. Thus was created Cultural Marxism, an idea so radical that it was rejected in Moscow. Eventually they were forced to flee Germany and were unfortunately granted a safe haven at Columbia University. Before long they had spread their views to most of the prominent universities in the country.

Cultural Marxism in academia would manifest itself in many ways. One such way was in the formation of the various ethnic, gender or sexual identity-based studies that litter the current curriculum. While the subjects of the studies differ, they are all essentially cloned versions of one another. The story is always the same, a minority group victimized by America and Western Civilization. The heroes change but the villains remain constantly, white, male and Christian. Critical Theory is applied to the various ways in which human beings characterize one another until all of human history is deconstructed so it can be rebuilt to fit the narrow lens of political correctness. The same process and principles used by earlier communists to reduce all of human history to a struggle between classes now being applied to the cultural identity of America. This leads to the creation of various victim groups which will later make up the majority coalition used to take over the country—otherwise known as the base of the Democratic Party. Their votes would be bought by the various perks and privileges offered up to them on the taxpayer's dime.

But these are not the people we are dealing with today. We are dealing with second and third generation Cultural Marxists that are the unfortunate byproduct of intellectual inbreeding—hired by, answering to, and surrounded by people holding the identical worldview. People that value "diversity" over merit and to whom the term "tolerance" means the mandatory and passionate embrace of political correctness. And they've dutifully passed on these values to the current generation of students.

Some of the grievances are legitimate, most notably slavery, but the degree to which it has been used to condemn our culture and history is an injustice in and of itself. First off, slaves were not exclusively African-American, and secondly history is full of war and conquest. Eventually, our culture and Constitution would bring a global evil to a fairly conclusive end. There are some places in the world where slavery is still accepted— but they are not a part of the Western world. And so in the end we have a group of enslaved people who were eventually liberated and granted citizenship by a society with a substantially higher standard of living, and who remain free to return to their ancestral homes if they so desire.

The remaining "victim" groups are primarily formed upon patently absurd premises, most notably victim-feminism, the true darling of political correctness. Victim-feminism, gender studies, women's studies, etc. take a hatchet to any and all areas of "male privilege" while completely ignoring areas of female privilege. These privileges being things such as their placement on the lifeboats of sinking ships ahead of men and their absence from the endless bloody battlefields spread across all of human history. Asymmetries between the sexes such as these are neglected in favor of remarkably less profound inequalities such as male dominance in the corporate world or double standards for sexual behavior. What *is* true is that men and women are biologically different and that societies historically arranged themselves in ways that accentuated the natural strengths of the two sexes. Thanks to technological advancements these expectations are often times no longer necessary for survival.

But political correctness does not call for a balanced discussion on allowing men and women to transcend their biological differences. Instead, one gender is encouraged to abandon their historical responsibilities to family, household and children while the other is eternally handicapped and shamed. This has had a devastating impact on the nuclear family which has been the *prime* target of Cultural Marxist deconstruction. A bicycle with one wheel removed won't take you anywhere and it can't even remain upright.

Curricula like these become the building blocks for even more absurd levels of deconstruction. If you need me to explain to you why sex and gender aren't social constructs I'm not sure this is the right book for you. Ideas like that don't belong in a classroom. Conversations of such absurd notions should be confined to small, windowless white rooms with padded walls.

The recently popularized transgender movement joins the mosaic of groups whom the Left alleges have been oppressed since the dawn of time. Never mind the fact that the medical technology required to appease the mentally ill by replacing their genetically dictated reproductive organs with prosthetic genitalia has only existed for about half a century. The purveyors of political correctness have no interest in facts; they are only interested in expanding the waistlines of people tipping their countries towards collapse.

Because these various social justice campaigns have no clearly defined endpoints they cannot accurately be referred to as equality movements. Groups aimed at endlessly expanding their own privilege while diminishing the rights and perceived privileges of others are more accurately described as supremacy movements.

The end result is a nation where the people unfortunate enough to resemble the ones who built it are consistently robbed of their lunch money while simultaneously being labeled as privileged oppressors.

The most popular buzzwords on the college campus are "tolerance" and "diversity." It quickly becomes evident that creating an environment conducive to learning takes a back seat to establishing an environment that promotes these new core values. By "diversity" they mean the tireless efforts to reduce admission rates of white men; and by tolerance they mean mandatory cheerleading for their politically correct worldview. This "tolerance" manifests itself as the creation of strict speech codes and the systematic and forceful removal of any conflicting viewpoints or ideas on these topics.

The omnipresent groupthink on the American campus did not occur overnight; the process has been gradual. Most of the smiling, do-good fascists found cheerfully enforcing PC orthodoxy on the campus have no idea that they are actively engaging in cultural terrorism. They are simply espousing the ideas they have been programmed to regurgitate; believing them to be the only ones acceptable for decent, moral and enlightened people. The end result is a place where students whose worldviews are informed by traditional Judeo-Christian values are constantly belittled or silenced either by subtle passive-aggressive bullying or direct intervention.

Through the creepy, in-house campus justice systems we see firsthand just how perverse our enemies' notions regarding justice and equality have become. As a general rule of thumb, when the Cultural Marxists call attention to a "war" on someone or something, look in the exact opposite direction to where they are pointing for the true victim. The prime example is the supposed "rape culture" and sexual victimization of women in college. While calling for an aggressive end to an alleged "epidemic" of sexual assaults against women, they have removed the due process rights of male students. Never mind that the stats used to justify this atrocious maneuvering are so heavily cooked that they're no longer safe for human consumption.

Campuses are aggressively littered with propaganda making absurd claims like "three out of four women will be victims of sexual assault at some point in their lives." Whenever someone dares to question these stats the ultimate answer is, "Who cares if we're too careful. Better safe than sorry." Never mind the fact that the inverse inference inevitably drawn from falsely asserting that three out of four women will be victims of sexual assault is that a significant proportion of men must be rapists. They talk about a dire need to end the all-pervasive "rape culture," and at some colleges greet all new female students with standard issued "rape whistles." Whistles that presumably operate exactly like traditional ones except that they can be figuratively blown weeks after engaging in consensual sex. The silent victims remain the countless young men who have had their lives destroyed by false allegations of rape and sexual assault.

Once again, the campus experience gets deconstructed and made to fit through the narrow lens of the applicable victim group dynamics of victim-feminism. What is in reality an "epidemic" of normal hormone-charged young adults getting drunk and having sex becomes a one-way epidemic of male sexual assault against women. This has led many states to enact shocking "yes means yes" initiatives which places the burden of proof in cases of alleged sexual assault on the accused and not the accuser. The Duke Lacrosse team can surely speak to the new paradigm, the cementing of which with hard policy is cause for great alarm. In cases of alleged sexual assault the expectation is now that the accused must produce a signed contract documenting the consent if they expect to be exonerated. Again, this is not hyperbole; it is policy. All brought to you by people constantly accusing their political opponents of obsessively pushing government into the bedroom.

Yes, the PC chickens have finally come home to roost at the original scene of the crime. Ultimately, what you are watching is the ugly death of the Academy. First and foremost it no longer offers education. It does not even offer an environment conducive to exploring ideas on your own, either. Hell, you can't even get laid in college anymore without a signed contract. Well, not unless you're willing to risk being accused of sexual assault by an angry ex-girlfriend a few weeks later and prepared to face prosecution by the college's gender tribunals, guilty until proven innocent.

On top of all of this, the cost of this dangerous and degrading experience is increasingly exorbitant. To paraphrase Matt Damon in *Goodwill Hunting*, you're much better off getting a library card. Or perhaps enrolling in an online course where you can get the knowledge and the credentials for a fraction of the cost with considerably less hassle. You'll also miss out on a heavy dosage of leftist brainwashing which has long been the primary function of academia. And that is precisely why I predict that this "free college" initiative from the Left will soon be the central item of the Democratic Party's platform. *Their survival as a party may well depend upon it.* Because we've given them unilateral control of education and they have utterly corrupted it, and because without the college campus there will be no one to train the next generation of Democratic voters. The cost of the atrocious product now being offered is simply not sustainable anymore, which is precisely why they will need to make it free, if not mandatory.

5

Political Correctness in Popular Culture

To see political correctness at work within popular culture one need only turn on the television. The values are so firmly entrenched within Hollywood that you wouldn't even notice they were there without having it pointed out. In much the sense that you don't consciously reflect on breathing air, most people are completely oblivious to the heavy leftist messaging found within virtually every channel save Fox News. Once again, we find victim-feminism front and center. It is virtually impossible, for example, to find a major television drama that does not contain the repudiation of male privilege as a central or subordinate theme. In sitcoms we laugh as the American family is humorously deconstructed before our very eyes. Where traditionally men were head of households we now find dad as an oafish, intellectually inferior creature who lives in constant fear of incurring the wrath of his wife. Of course, mom and dad kiss and make up in the end but only after dad's scheme is foiled by his own bumbling ineptitude. In comedies focusing on single and dating life we have the now classic routine where guy says something awkward to girl which is followed by an awkward pause which is followed by girl slapping guy in the face which is followed by cued laughter. This particular routine has become commonplace in children's movies as well. Animated Disney movies, for example, love to show strong girls humorously beating up clumsy boys. This is interesting because our historic cultural sensitivity to violence perpetrated by men against women stems from the understanding that it is "not a fair fight." Disney, meanwhile is telling an entire generation of young children that not only are women more powerful than men, but that it is actually funny when a girl hits a boy, and this is often simply a normal expression of flirtatious behavior.

Even films designed primarily for men such as comic book style action movies are filled with similar dynamics. It has apparently become mandatory, for example, for there to be at least one scene per movie where the female heroine demonstrates that her physical prowess is not only equal to her male counterparts but that it exceeds it. The slap to the face gag is also routinely used in these movies to provide moments of levity. These narrative techniques are now clichéd so the envelope is pressed further with the current trend being to replace the male heroes entirely with female protagonists.

Last year Disney, a company once revered for wholesome, family entertainment, released a superb example of cinematic deconstruction in the movie *Maleficent*. It deconstructs the story of Snow White. The wicked witch for whom the movie is named is revealed to be the heroine, while the villain turns out to be the wicked white man who betrayed and figuratively raped her in her youth. Even when history reveals the most extreme examples of female privilege such as when men surrendered their seats on lifeboats to women as the Titanic sank to the bottom of the ocean, Hollywood still manages to find an angle from which to attack male privilege. In *Titanic*, as Rose's mother tightens her daughter's corset while sternly urging her to accept the subservient role society forces her onto as a woman, it becomes impossible to deny how plainly feminism misses the forest for the trees. In a fitting nod to victim-feminism, this same character is entirely mum when she becomes one of the very first passengers privileged enough to be placed on one of the limited number of lifeboats.

Another prevalent theme in film and television is the glorification of homosexuality and transgenderism. The quickest way to gain consideration for awards and accolades is to feature homosexuality as brave, noble or persecuted—preferably all three.   Sitcoms are full of loving depictions of homosexuals, and competitive reality shows feature gay and lesbian contestants at rates far in excess of their actual representation in the general population. I recently stumbled upon a dad-themed episode of a cooking battle show wherein two of the four contestants were gay. The justification of this promotion by the media moguls is that they are presenting a more "realistic" representation of the cultural landscape. This is a bald-faced lie. They are presenting *their* idealized version of the country, one even more thoroughly deconstructed than the one we live in today. They're not coming at it from a place of wanting to stand up for two percent of the population. They're coming at it from a place of wanting to make two percent, twenty percent, forty percent, or as high a number as they possibly can.

Popular music, historically rebellious in nature, gets in on the act as well. Feminism and sexual liberation are popular themes as sexed-up teenage girls mimic strip dancers to the adulation of their fans. We also see a rare acceptance of chauvinism when mostly African-American rappers refer to women as "bitches and hos" while waving guns around. The messaging from the music industry is not quite as uniform as we find in other forms of media, but it certainly falls under the umbrella of a culture celebrating its own demise.

At first glance, the prevalence of this handful of themes would seem highly bizarre. If men are biologically predisposed to physicality, why would every action movie include a demonstration of the superior strength of a woman? Much like in academia, the people creating this phenomenon are not fully cognizant of what they are doing. The irrationality can only be explained by understanding the programming. First and foremost, every college educated American is trained to apply critical theory to their field and to deconstruct it. It therefore follows that when a filmmaker approaches a genre historically dominated by men their first impulse is to emasculate. The uniformity of the phenomenon is testament to the thoroughness of their indoctrination. Political correctness issues a challenge to its devotees to create a world as diametrically opposite to Nature as possible. When one understands this equation their behavior becomes easy to predict. Give a Cultural Marxist a dollhouse and they will give it to a boy, give them a basketball and they will give it to a girl.

This same rule applies to the News networks (excluding Fox News), and it starts with story selection. The world is vast and an infinite number of events occur each day. Prior to the rise of political correctness, news organizations did their best to filter out the most significant events and present them to the public. Contemporary mainstream media now prioritizes narrative over significance and seeks first to present stories that reaffirm their distorted view of reality. This is why the countless examples of black-on-black or black-on-white crime go uncovered. Instead, an African-American criminal who is shot and killed while charging at a cop in the midst of a crime spree gets wall-to-wall coverage. Often times the degree to which reality is stretched to fit their desired narrative is comical. When new evidence emerges that contradicts the original portrayal the story is retired rather than corrected. Mainstream media networks such as CNN that attempt to present both sides usually do so only by presenting strawman conservative arguments they can easily disparage. You will be hard-pressed, for example, to find a conservative explaining that marriage was created to address the wellbeing of the child born from male and female sexuality. Instead, you will be treated to numerous Bible-thumpers quoting scripture. Once again, it's the same phenomenon we find in academia and popular culture: Trained cultural terrorists deconstructing their chosen medium until they can transmute it into their Bizarro-world reality. The success of Fox News is proof that nature abhors a vacuum. All the people who rejected the mainstream media's filtering news through the lens of political correctness flocked to the network, making it the industry leader. This is not to say that Fox News doesn't have its own agenda, which it most certainly does. Their colossal ratings dominance is merely a consequence of the fact that there is no one else in town remotely interested in competing for conservative viewership.

Now, even sports, a place where Americans could always turn for a true, unscripted and pure experience, has become co-opted by political correctness.

It's been nearly 29 years since Heidi Russo made the decision to give her son up for adoption. In 2013, a five minute segment aired on ESPN's *SportsCenter* about Mrs. Russo and the decision she made regarding Colin Kaepernick. The piece revealed that at the age of 18 Mrs.

Russo became pregnant with the son of a man who "made it very clear" that he wanted nothing to do with his child. She then explains her decision to carry Colin into the world before giving him up for adoption to people that could provide him with all of the things she thought a child would need—these things being financial stability and a mother and a father.

The Kaepernicks already had two sons but were looking to add a third to their family; specifically a bi-racial boy, something Mrs. Russo admits struck her as "interesting." Luckily for Colin, his father was African-American which meant that he qualified to join the family and their upper middle-class community.

The decision to put Colin up for adoption was clearly a difficult one for Mrs. Russo, who becomes emotional during the segment. It couldn't have been an easy choice for an 18-year-old single mother to make. The alternative choices she faced were either to raise Colin as a single mother or to terminate the pregnancy, as the father (who to this day refuses to be identified) presumably would have preferred. Faced with a tough decision it's entirely possible that she made the decision that was simultaneously best for her son and the most painful for herself.

Last week Colin Kaepernick, now NFL's highest paid backup quarterback made headlines by refusing to stand during the national anthem. He later addressed his actions (which he'd apparently been doing all pre-season) stating that he was "not going to stand up to show pride in a flag for a country that oppresses black people and people of color."

The story created quite a stir and the NFL reacted swiftly, although not the way one might expect from a league fresh off of a successful two-year legal battle to suspend their poster boy, Tom Brady, a quarter of the season for under-inflated footballs. Shockingly, within a day the NFL, 49ers and their coach had all issued virtually identical statements that signaled that he would not be punished for the incident. Other players, coaches and NFL alumni would weigh in on the controversy as well, each saying essentially the same thing. Citing the First Amendment, everyone seemed to agree that while they respected the national anthem, so too did they respect Kaepernick's right to free speech. This week it has come out that Kaepernick has also apparently been wearing socks that feature cartoon pigs dressed as cops. Every indication thus far is that this too, will go unpunished.

There's something hilarious about watching the same social justice warriors who ran other icons like Curt Schilling and Mike Ditka out of the sports world suddenly become constitutional scholars to defend a low-life like Colin Kaepernick. We expect such childishness from intellectual children but it's always disappointing when the adults in the room choose to play along with them.

Of course Kaepernick's speech is protected by the First Amendment. That's why he's not sitting in a prison or being lined up in front of a firing squad. The First Amendment is not however, nor has it ever been understood to be a blank check to say and do what you like at work without fear of losing your job. Freedom of speech exists to protect you from courtrooms—not the workplace expectations of your employer.

To appreciate the absurdity of applying the First Amendment to Kaepernick's behavior one need only apply the same logic to any other workplace dispute. Let's say for example, that you work at McDonald's. A customer notices that you appear unhappy or disgruntled and asks you why? You reply that you're unhappy because you work for a corrupt corporation that exploits and underpays its employees while delivering food to the masses that is unfit for human consumption. Your boss overhears your conversation, steps in and defends the McDonald's brand to the customer before handing him his food and wishing him a nice day. He then calls you into his office—and does *absolutely nothing*. Why? Because your boss respects your freedom of speech, that's why.

Clearly, it's absurd. In both cases.

The NFL itself has a long history of disciplining players and coaches for exercising their freedom of speech when it's perceived as detrimental to the league's image. You know, like the countless times coaches have been fined for criticizing officials. Or when Chad "Ochocinco" got fined for wearing a gold jacket which read "future hall of famer" on the sidelines. How about the time they investigated the entire Dolphins organization because Richie Incognito allegedly used a racial slur at a night club? Or when Marshawn Lynch got fined for simply refusing to say anything at all during press conferences? Wasn't he just "pleading the Fifth?"

Because the NFL clearly understands that the First Amendment does not prohibit them from using disciplinary actions to dictate the conduct of their employees, the only conclusion to be reached from their refusal to punish Kaepernick is that his comments do not in fact contradict the values of their brand. Remember also, that just last month another player, Isaiah Crowell tweeted a graphic depiction of a police officer being beheaded by a militant Black Panther. Not only did the league not discipline him for the deplorable tweet but they refused to even acknowledge it as a story on NFL.com.

Like the NBA, which recently decided to pull its all-star game from North Carolina because the state does not allow men to use women's restrooms, the NFL has clearly signaled their surrender to and compliance with politically correct fascism. Kaepernick drew a clear line in the sand and the NFL cannot have it both ways. When your employee insults your customer as Kaepernick did yours, you must make a choice. It is a widely accepted business practice of siding with your customer, who "is always right." This is especially true in a case like this, where your employee has chosen to insult your customer without provocation. These are the core concepts of what is understood as customer service but unfortunately they have no place in a business governed by political correctness and identity politics. Under those principles the NFL is far more likely to discipline a player for not wearing enough pink during breast cancer awareness month than they are to discipline Kaepernick for wearing cartoon pig cops on his feet. The NFL has a long and storied history of saluting our military but as we've seen time and time again, political correctness is a jealous lover who refuses to take the backseat to anything or anyone, including our national anthem. By refusing to discipline Kaepernick, the NFL, the 49ers and everyone associated with the league that lacked the courage to condemn his actions are acting as his accomplices. The league's statement also serves as a green light to his peers that they are free to join him. One of Kaepernick's team mates, Eric Reid has already done so. Others will no doubt soon follow suit. Kaepernick and Reid are responsible for their actions—but just as Obama bears responsibility for the "Ferguson effect" so too will the NFL ultimately be responsible for the "Kaepernick effect."

You've probably guessed by now that I don't like Colin Kaepernick. Truth be told, I've never really liked him. Why not? Simply put, I don't like the way he looks or presents himself. To each their own but I'm just not a fan of the tattoos-head-to-toe, backwards-baseball-cap and gigantic-headphones-around-the-neck look. And no, that's not a race thing. My favorite athlete of all-time is Michael Jordan. Growing up I had it all, Jordan posters, jerseys, you name it. Jordan is regarded as one of the greatest athletes in history of all sports. Michael Jordan also happened to have not one but two African-American parents and grew up in a predominantly black neighborhood. He also spoke proper English and didn't show up at press conferences dressed like he was about to rob a 7/11. He chose to present himself to the world as a winner and that's exactly what he was and will always be. Kaepernick is a loser who chooses to present himself to the world as a thug. And no, that's not a racial dog whistle. The term "thug" has historical significance as a description of a lifestyle, attitude and method for procuring money and power through force and intimidation. The reason why the term is frequently associated with the African-American community is because African-American men frequently seek out the term as a source of status.

"Thuggery" did not originate in the African-American community, nor is it the only place that it is found.

Thuggery is also the preferred modus operandi for Muslim extremist groups such as ISIS. To be fair, Kaepernick isn't really a thug. He's actually just a thug wannabe. The great irony is that he did not forge his fashion, attitudes or ideas on the street. His only connection to the urban, African-American community is an absent father he has never spoken to who would have preferred he'd never been born. Kaepernick's politics and worldview were taught to him by the affluent white progressives who specifically adopted him to add "diversity" to their household. The fact that his girlfriend is a Black Lives Matter activist who convinced him to convert to Islam likely did not help.

In Kaepernick we see several abominable movements coalescing into one exponentially more offensive and destructive package. In him we see the inevitable blending of black power thuggery with Islamic thuggery—both cultivated and empowered by liberal white-guilt.

There are 114 million reasons for Kaepernick to stand during our national anthem but he is far too lost to ever recognize a single one of them. The problem with false narratives is that once they succeed in disconnecting a person from reality it becomes impossible to ever make their world whole again. There is nothing that anyone can do to remedy the injustice Kaepernick perceives because it doesn't actually exist. Kaepernick is an ignorant and immature young man who is making a stand against things like "hands up don't shoot" that never actually happened. The next time Kaepernick meets with the media to lecture Americans on privilege remember that he likely wouldn't even be alive if the culture he chooses to identify with had controlled his destiny. In the urban thug culture, it is customary for bastard children like him to be terminated before they are born. Remember also that he was selected by his white, well-to-do adopted family specifically because of his mixed ethnicity. Remember too, that in spite of the fact that he has known none of the socio-economic hardships linked to the African-American community he nonetheless by birthright retains the coveted status of victimhood. A status that grants him the privilege to insult you, your country and the people that defend it live on television without any fear of punishment. Remember all of that the next time the NFL pretends to stand with our military, police or flag as well.

# # #

6

The Democratic Party Makes a Deal with the Devil

The election of Barack Obama in 2008 is considered historic because he is the first African-American president. His election is actually historic for a much more profound reason: he was the first president elected by a majority coalition devoted to the values of political correctness.

The partnership between the Democratic Party and Cultural Marxists had been forged decades earlier, but Obama became the first U.S. President to be elected as a result of that partnership. Not only did they intend for Obama to be the first president elected by this coalition but it is their intention to make George W Bush the last U.S. president elected by Americans with traditional values. Their intent is for their new, ever expanding majority to rise out of and forever away from the ashes of the America envisioned by our founding fathers. If a sharp correction is not made, and quickly, they will likely achieve their objective.

The precise moment when the partnership began isn't clear but I have come to believe that it occurred somewhere around the time Richard Nixon became president. By then the Cultural Marxists had been lurking around the college campus for some thirty-odd years and found their perfect disciples in the flower children of the sixties. The sixties generation had been brought up in an age of unprecedented middle-class comfort and security. Their security in hand, they even had the luxury of growing bored with the safety-net cultivated for them by their hard-working parents. The combination of this mindset with powerful, mind-altering substances would make the hippies the ideal foot soldiers to fight the first battle in what would eventually become the Culture War.

The advent of television and its coverage of the Vietnam War meant that for the first time in our history civilians were seeing the horrors of war with their own eyes. The media was reporting on stories in ways that may have conflicted with our national security interests. The communists fanned the flames of war into an explosion of anti-war protest which emerged from the universities into the streets. Though Nixon had not started the war he became its face. The scorn that Nixon received from both a rabid media and America's youth was ferocious and unprecedented. Whether or not it was the impetus for Nixon's paranoia it clearly contributed to the state of mind that would later prove to be his undoing. In this moment a new dynamic was formed in American politics, one wherein the media, popular culture and academic institutions began to work jointly against a common enemy. Earlier in the decade Cultural Marxism had also played a role in encouraging racial riots and unrest. It was a time when Saul Alinsky's "Rules for Radicals" was considered a very hip book to read. The various seeds of political correctness were coming to maturity and coalescing against the leader of the country. But there was one element missing, the movement lacked a meaningful presence in politics. Naturally, since the Republicans were in power the Democratic Party had a vested interest in seeing Nixon torn down. As today's Republican Party becomes the de facto party for patriots, the Democrats became the de facto party of people opposed to the war... ironic, since it had been started by a Democratic president.

The historic take-down of Nixon could not have occurred without the assistance of the media and the Cultural Marxists. Though it's hard to imagine that the Democrats of the day grasped the gravity of what they had done, they nevertheless had wittingly colluded with cultural terrorism against a sitting president. It was the first of what would prove to be many mutually beneficial victories shared by the communists and the Democratic Party. Though the Marxists may have had a natural inclination towards the blue collar tendencies of the Democratic Party, they likely didn't care much that Nixon was a Republican, only that he was President. Had the sitting president been a Democrat it's entirely possible that the same transaction may have occurred in reverse. Regardless, the partnership was formed and a dynamic between the parties began that endures to this day.

From then on the Democratic Party became the advocate for the various victim groups created by the Cultural Marxists. The struggle between blue and white collar workers devolved into a discussion over whether or not to deconstruct America. The Democrats had purchased stock amongst women and minorities and began supporting policies to raise the value of those stocks while simultaneously devaluing the voice of a predominantly white country.

Next, we begin this crazy struggle over questioning whether or not we should have functional borders, and turning our immigration system into a political weapon. We see our welfare programs rearranged from ones aimed at reinforcing the nuclear family into ones that incentivize their destruction. Handouts being awarded to individuals with alternate lifestyles and destructive behaviors. Under the guise of promoting diversity we see a rigorous handicapping apparatus installed across many aspects of society such as college admissions and workplace hirings. All of these changes being championed by the Left.

Many of these policy changes are blatantly discriminatory against whites, and specifically designed to alter the demography of the country. The Democrats begin borrowing the sales tactics of the Cultural Marxists to disguise their objectives in order to keep the rate of white flight out of the party below the rate of the expansion of minority groups. Historically, political parties craft platforms designed to appeal to various groups in order to form majority coalitions. The Democratic Party works in reverse, employing a tactic I refer to as "electorate shaping" wherein they support policies designed to reshape the country into supporting their politics.

# # #

7

The Silent Revolution

The process didn't occur overnight, but by 2008 the Democratic Party reaped the plentiful bounty of the harvest planted forty-some-odd years before. Half of the nation's children are raised in broken homes, most of which rely heavily upon government assistance for survival. A thoroughly broken immigration system has led to a massive shift in the country's demographics. Two generations of educated adults have been funneled through indoctrination camps masquerading as educational institutions. Many Americans are generally disoriented, broken and largely dysfunctional. The younger half of the country accepts the deconstructed worldview as normal without batting an eye. Cultural Marxism has morphed into an independent, organic monstrosity with a life and mind of its own. It has become the monster that is political correctness, a beast whose tentacles permeate nearly every aspect of daily American life. On top of all this, the country has just sat through eight years of an atrocious Republican presidency that reached a crescendo with the massive financial crisis and "Great Recession." And so when confronted with a choice between an articulate African-American raised in the Third World by communist revolutionaries and Muslims and an old white male known for his incredible heroism in the Vietnam War... well, you know the rest.

Now in 2015, nearing the end of Obama's second term as president we begin to understand his legacy. Most disappointingly, a man elected with an unspoken assumption from do-good Caucasians that he would forever pardon them of their white guilt has... done the opposite. Our now twice-elected black president has taken every opportunity to exacerbate racial tensions. The white electorate that voted in hopes of a post-racial America was proven to be wildly naive. What could they realistically have expected from the Democratic Party? Remember the lesson earlier about the principle of deconstruction. Give the Cultural Marxists *Snow White* and they will repay you with *Maleficent*. Give them a country and they will, well... destroy it!

To be fair to Obama, he is not some ideologically unique monster. In fact, he is ideologically quite similar to virtually every other member of his party. As a black man his contempt for whites might have more bite than Hillary Clinton's cynical solidarity with Black America, but her personal, seething contempt for men makes them more or less equivalent. He is the symptom, not the cause: the benefactor of the unholy alliance between radical communists and the Democratic Party. He has done a good job for them and expanded many of the operational tactics that had previously only been possible on the college campus. Most notably, we see the implementation of what I refer to as the "Obama doctrine." If a conflict can be deconstructed to fit the lens of identity politics—that is to say if Obama can argue persecution of a protected victim group—then rule of law becomes irrelevant. The executive branch may then move unilaterally to come to their perceived defense. This is a *perceived* defense because as we established earlier, when Cultural Marxists claim someone or something is under attack—the reverse is usually true. Therefore, the Obama doctrine is primarily used as a sword rather than a shield.

He has also proven to be a creative pioneer when it comes to the Left's favorite hobby: deconstruction. By setting the keen eye of the federal government on law enforcement he has deconstructed the crime data and the staggeringly disproportionate amount of violent crime committed by African-Americans. The conclusion drawn is predictable. It's the one opposite to reality. Give a Cultural Marxist data showing thirteen percent of a population being responsible for half of its murders and they will conclude that the cause of the disparity is racist laws and racist enforcement of the law. Rather than putting effort and energy into encouraging the mending of a broken community, energy and resources are applied to "correct" our criminal justice system. As political correctness rolls into law enforcement it crosses the line from severely hassling whites to placing them in danger— as local law enforcement will be under increasing pressure to simultaneously look the other way at minority crime while looking for opportunities to arrest whites. This movement, spearheaded by the leadership of Attorney General Eric Holder successfully converts law enforcement into a political weapon.

We recently learned that Obama has been collecting an unprecedented racial database pertaining to all aspects of civilian life which he plans to release to the public as a parting gift before leaving office. The massive treasure trove of data will provide decades of fodder for the social justice warriors to deconstruct and convert into political weapons against whites. Obama knows that the best way to protect the Left's investment in the tearing down of America is to create new tools to be used for deconstructive purposes. While I shrink from comparing anyone to Adolf Hitler, you would have to go back to Nazi Germany before finding a Western leader more obsessed with race than Obama. Thankfully, the motives of our current, racially obsessed leadership have our best interest in mind, right? And then there's the weaponization of the IRS against conservatives under Obama. Most everywhere you look the Obama administration can be found applying teeth that will be used by the "deep state" to attack the values of traditional Americans long after his administration ends.

We also see the projection of political correctness onto foreign policy. Because many believe Obama is a Muslim his actions create a bizarre paradox. Does Obama refuse to refer to Islamic terrorists as what they are—terrorists committing atrocities and mayhem in the name of their religion, *Islam*—because his politically correct conditioning informs him to protect those seeking to harm America? Or does Obama embrace political correctness because as a Muslim he recognizes Islamacist ideology for the anti-Western weapon that it is? It's an interesting question but not one that this book aims to answer. The end result of Obama's foreign policy is the weakening of our influence and the stability of our alliances, while those seeking to harm us are empowered and emboldened. Because this is consistent with the principle of deconstruction as the common thread connecting the various tentacles of political correctness, it is safe to assume this outcome is deliberate. Is it really any surprise that when Islamic terrorists attacked our embassy in Benghazi and killed four Americans the first instinct of those is charge was to deconstruct the story until they could find a way to blame Americans for it?

# # #

8

What Now?

At this point you're probably asking yourself "How did we let them get away with this?" It's a good question and one I often ask myself. I think the simplest answer is that the Republican Party and conservatives as a whole simply didn't grasp what was happening. To this day I see many conservative politicians and pundits that clearly don't have a clue. While they're certainly more aware than they were say, ten years ago, a majority of prominent conservatives still don't really *get* it. First and foremost, the entire conservative movement from the grassroots to Mitch McConnell needs to be "debriefed" on political correctness and Cultural Marxism.

While the cancer of political correctness has metastasized throughout the body of Western Civilization, it has unfortunately failed to spread to our enemies. Cultural Marxism and the desire of countries to denigrate and reduce their predominant ethnic groups, customs and values don't play particularly well in the Middle East. Most of the leaders in that part of the world are more concerned with annihilating anyone who doesn't look, act and believe exactly as they do. Westerners made to feel embarrassed because they too closely resemble the people that built their nations cannot expect to be greeted as comrades-in-arms should they attempt to flee. I am not aware of any academic grants or workplace initiatives in China that specifically target individuals that aren't of Chinese descent and who don't speak their language and follow their social mores etc. There is no reciprocal rolling out of the red carpet to be found for Westerners outside of Europe and the US. What sane civilization would ever go out of its way to court the disintegration of any and everything that unites its people? No, escape is not an option. The only options left are to take it in the shorts, day by day until your tribe's voice is entirely snuffed out... or to take part in an effort to rid your country and community of this fatal affliction.

To restate the mission statement of this book, it is intended to do two things. The first part provides a brief explanation of what we are up against. The portion that follows aims to get everyone on the same page and organize a coherent resistance movement. In the closing chapters we will outline strategies for how to individually battle political correctness in three aspects of life: first as private citizen, second as media creator and third as politician. These roles build upon themselves sequentially, that is to say it is my goal to encourage you to start as a citizen patriot, become a creator of media and then perhaps enter the political arena yourself. But before we can do that we must begin by taking inventory of ourselves.

# # #

9

Political Correctness as Mental Illness

Because political correctness frequently (and deliberately) robs individuals of their capacity to reason logically we can consider political correctness a mental illness. Those afflicted with the disease have had a thought mechanism installed in their brain that closely mirrors dyslexia. Just as the instincts of a dyslexic are to read backwards, a properly brainwashed PC twit instinctively views most moral or intellectual questions from a similarly backwards perspective. Unfortunately because today's psychiatrists are more concerned with diagnosing energetic kids with "Attention Deficit Disorder" and confused ones with various gender identity disorders, most people suffering from political correctness will never have it brought to their attention. While the link between liberalism and political correctness is profound, classifying yourself as a conservative does not mean you are immune to the condition. Below is a sample question that ten out of the eleven leading Republicans presidential hopefuls got wrong during a recent political debate. Let's see how you stack up!

<u>Pop Quiz: Do You Suffer From Political Correctness?</u>

Question: *Which woman would you like to see replace Alexander Hamilton on the $10 bill?*

A) Rosa Parks

B) Your Wife

C) Mother Theresa

D) Your Mother

Answer: It's a trick question. The gender of the person selected to be featured on our currency is irrelevant. Deciding to pick a woman first, before determining the merit of the selection is inherently discriminatory and anti-American. If we are to add new faces to our currency it should be consistent with our national tradition of featuring important historical figures who have served as national leaders. As such, it will be appropriate to feature a woman on our currency when America produces a female politician or president who history proves to be as influential as men like George Washington and Benjamin Franklin. I encourage Cultural Marxists to form their own country where they would be welcome to assign one currency denomination to each identity group they consider a victim class. In America however, we celebrate *accomplishment*, so please defile someone else's currency with your intellectual graffiti.

Ironically the only person on stage who got the question right at the time was the only woman on stage. We're fortunate to have women like Carly Fiorina in the Republican Party who prefer recognition for being correct rather than for being a woman. Meanwhile, every man on the stage including purportedly anti-PC candidates like Cruz, Trump and Carson all failed the test. That's because in this particular moment they all instinctively saw the question as an opportunity to prove how pro-women they were. It's the exact same mentality that led Romney to make his infamous "binders full of women" response to a similarly themed question about "gender equality." The men were all so afraid of being labeled by the media as "anti-women" that not a single one of them bothered to ask why on earth would we make a selection based upon gender first and merit second? This incident shows why it is false to claim that political correctness only controls the Left. While political correctness may manifest itself differently in the parties it is clearly present in both. The

Democratic Party is controlled by positive reinforcement, like a dog walking perfectly in stride with its master. The Republican Party is controlled by fear, like a dog whimpering in the corner who knows not to wag its tail lest it risk receiving another beating at the hand of its master. As Romney learned first-hand, even the deferential cowardly conservative dog inevitably gets beaten anyway.

Because the condition has been injected deep within the impulse functions of our brains, ridding yourself of the affliction requires patience and dedication. Some may only need a gentle nudge and a slight course correction, but if you are Stage 4 you should safely assume that your views are 180 degrees out of phase with reality. The only way to treat cases such as these is by committing yourself to the "Opposite George" method (google *Seinfeld*), the practice of embracing the viewpoint or idea that seems counter-intuitive when choosing a course of action in a social setting. Rejecting or Opposite-Georging your faulty programming by applying a 180 degree shift, you complete the circle back to reality and over time, your head should emerge from out of your ass.

# # #

10

Attacking Political Correctness as a Private Citizen

The first thing you need to be aware of is that opposing political correctness is moderately dangerous and may soon become lethal unless it is arrested. Being flagged as a conservative, particularly on cultural issues, may cost you your job, reputation and friends. As a private citizen I recommend separating your life as an activist from your life as a functional member of society. In your daily duties you should be respectful and reserved, especially pertaining to political conversations. You will likely hear a lot of PC nonsense at the water cooler, and if you do, resist the urge to butt in. Regardless of politically correct etiquette, politics should not be discussed at work unless with people you are sufficiently close to. One of the most obnoxious things about the politically correct is their lack of basic civility and class. The best example of this lack of professionalism is once again found in universities where many of the liberal professors have the appalling habit of sharing their views with impressionable students in courses that have nothing to do with politics. They do this because they can, because all their peers have the same views and because they are arrogant enough to view their lack of professionalism as civil service.

Don't stoop to their level. When these losers make disparaging remarks about conservatives or Republicans without bothering to check if anyone in the room happens to identify as one, the best course of action is to generally ignore them. As you form friendships in the workplace you can feel your way around to see where they stand on issues. Occasionally you might make a friend who is politically neutral. A clever comment can help steer them in the right direction without even seeming political.

Example:

> Bill: *Did you get your paycheck yet?*
>
> Patriot: *Yeah man, couldn't believe how much of it went to taxes. So depressing.*
>
> Bill: *Oh I know man, I hate taxes.*
>
> Patriot: *Well, someone's gotta pay for all this crap Obama is doing.*
>
> Bill: *Heh. Yeah.*
>
> Patriot: *What's for lunch?*

That's it, a little innocent banter. Short and sweet. If "Bill" shares your views it's likely he'll push forward with the conversation. If he doesn't, just move on and continue with your business. If there's an overtly conservative co-worker, resist the urge to join in with him unless you are in a position of total security or authority. Instead, in private make light of the fact that you prefer to fly under the radar, with a low profile. Share your views with him or her privately but make sure to remind him that you don't want everyone in the office knowing where you stand. These are tips coming from a guy that has spent his entire life in California and Massachusetts. You may not need to be this careful if you're in a red state but I can tell you first hand that if your superiors are liberal and find out about your conservative views they will almost certainly treat you less fairly moving forward. Remember, these are people who are trained to aggressively attack and reject any ideas that contradict their programming. As a general rule, if a person lacks the professionalism to keep their views private then they will inversely lack the professionalism to recognize someone else's differing views and treat them fairly.

The name of the game for a citizen patriot is handling your business and tending to your own. As a general rule of thumb seek out employment opportunities in the private sector over taking a government job or anything remotely attached to the welfare apparatus. If you're looking for rewarding work and haven't settled on a career I recommend working in sales over hourly or even lower-end salaried positions. The reason for this is simple: careers in sales provide you with more ownership of your paycheck, and because it is a results-driven field it is harder for political correctness to dictate the terms. Political correctness is good at many things such as rewarding cronyism but it proves to be far from effective in a business environment. When applying for an hourly or salaried position the success of your application and future advancement within the corporation will always be tied to identity politics, meaning your race, gender and sexual orientation. Because employment positions like these (especially in the public sector) value social deconstruction over production, these jobs tend to be less rewarding and generally place a ceiling on your earning potential.

If you happen to be a minority these opportunities might seem appealing. However, even the recipients of the politically correct "gifts" will ultimately be held back from reaching their full potential by accepting work on a dysfunctional, sinking ship. Admittedly, the pensions and retirement plans aren't nearly as fluffy in the private sector, but whenever possible you want to put your work in line with the part of the country that is working and driving the economy and away from the dysfunctional cronyism of political correctness. Working in the private sector has the added perk of reducing the likelihood of working with liberals, as they generally find themselves unequipped to succeed in a results-driven career—not to mention politically correct employment practices mandated by the State in the public sector are inherently contradictory to the profit motive.

In your personal life you want to do your best to be good and honorable in the meaningful relationships that define you. One of the main reasons why the deconstruction of the family is such a crucial component of the Left's political agenda is because an intact family is the first line of defense against government dependency. A family led by a committed mother and father partnership is demonstrably more likely to produce self-sufficient children who will contribute to society rather than leech off of it. This simple fact, by the way, is the basis for the institution of marriage as defined between man and woman. Self-sufficiency is no friend to the cause of political correctness. Political correctness prefers the promotion of alternatives such as the single-mother household. In this model, the father (often criminalized) is removed from the home and converted into a virtual slave-worker for the new household. Secondly, one home is converted into two. The emphasis is then placed upon maintaining the standard of living of the home where mom and children live. You're splitting something apart and then expecting one half to maintain both halves. Even the massive amount of child support taken from the father often proves insufficient, so the rest of the burden is absorbed by the taxpayer. The standard of living for the father's household is considered irrelevant, which contributes to the alarming rates of male homelessness. In the absence of a father figure mom and kids (often from multiple fathers) become perpetually reliant upon government for assistance. It therefore follows that they will always view political efforts seeking to rescind the role of government and advocating for personal responsibility in an adversarial light. All of this made possible by a rapacious family court system and anti-male domestic violence regime that routinely starts the process by criminalizing men for spanking their children or for having an argument with their spouse.

I myself am the product of a broken home and have seen first-hand the destructive impact it can have on the entire family. Ironically, the person most harmed by the divorce in my family turned out to be my dear mother. Largely due to the great care in which both of my parents took in raising and educating my brother and I, I'm fortunate to have emerged from relative poverty to a life of great comfort. My mother however, once a highly accomplished physics student attending NYU was never able to find employment that matched her intellectual capacity. Today it is my pleasure to be in a position to support her. I reconcile my troubled childhood by realizing that I have two amazing parents whom I love and who deeply love me. I view what we all endured as the consequence of a societal collapse and have made it my aim to push back against that collapse rather than to perpetuate it. The fundamental question I face is whether or not I want to celebrate other broken homes so that I may feel more "normal" or whether to speak truthfully about the consequences of deconstructing the traditional family and hope that others will avoid the things mine could not. This becomes a defining difference between conservatives and liberals.

There is nothing Leftists love more than finding personal dirt on conservatives to paint them as hypocrites. The truth is none of us are perfect, everyone makes mistakes. Making mistakes does not disqualify a person from expressing an opinion; in fact doing so is a sign of maturity. Just because you're a recovered alcoholic doesn't mean you should strive for prohibition on all alcohol consumption. There's a fundamental question we all face when we make a mistake. Do I want to promote a world that diminishes the likelihood of others making my mistakes or do I want to promote a world that perpetuates these mistakes so that I might feel more comfortable in it? A wise man once said "Let he who hath not sinned cast the first stone." This is a very powerful statement but it is one that the Left has twisted to fit their ideology. After Jesus defended Mary Magdalene he does not then go on to encourage her to continue with her life as a prostitute, nor does he encourage others to join her. He doesn't just empathize with her mistakes. He picks her up with compassion and shows her a better way. The ideal here is to strive for a world absent of both stone and "sin." Social progressivism seeks to do something entirely different. It elevates Mary Magdalene to the rank of sainthood and encourages the shaming of any who don't actively promote, support or participate in her behavior. It seeks to turn the entire dynamic of morality upon its head.

The objective here is not the removal of stones from society but rather to take them out of the hands of those who strive to uphold standards of personal conduct and place them into the hands of those that don't. In other words, the concept of morality has not been removed from the equation, it has merely been redefined. The redefinition is achieved by reversing the positions of that which once was deemed good and virtuous with that which was not. In this paradigm, it is not sufficient to simply live and let live. The line in the sand used to separate good people from bad is the agreement with the behaviors deemed "good" by the liberal fascist authority. By taking the mantle of normalcy these elitists seek to alleviate the nagging discomfort of their conscience by encouraging others to emulate their behavior. This is the social and cultural landscape of Western Civilization circa 2015. It's a utopian world for people seeking to silence that voice from within, and a prison for those that seek to learn from and connect with it. Misery loves company and in this brave new world the only shame is shame itself.

The role of the social conservative as private citizen becomes clear: to promote your values by doing your best to live by them. And where you fail to measure up to your own moral standard—get up and try again. I've discovered that the more time you take to get to know a person the harder it becomes to dislike them. If you see fault in the ways of your neighbor don't rush to lecture him. Instead, maintain a consistent stance of love and compassion. If in time you build a true friendship, you may be surprised to find them asking for your advice someday

As political correctness continues the systematic dismantling of our country you will find yourself increasingly crossing paths with people you know are engaged in behaviors you don't agree with. This is by design. Liberals argue that homosexuality is a birth trait and as such work to defend a small percentage of the population from oppressive social mores. However, their policies seem to suggest a belief in nurture vs nature. Therefore the politically correct answer to the "nature vs nurture" debate seems to be the nurturing of the unnatural. We can clearly see the goal of political correctness is not to protect a finite percentage of homosexuals but rather to make the percentage of citizens engaged in homosexuality as large as possible. They are doing this because they want everyone to have a loved one who identifies as a homosexual. They want Republicans like Dick Cheney and Rob Portman to have gay children. By spreading the degeneration they gradually convince everyone in society to "evolve" on the issue out of compassion for a loved one. The false choice presented is the choice to love or hate your family and friends.

You can love your child without agreeing with their guidance counselor's suggestion that he or she undergo gender reassignment surgery, an irreversible procedure that permanently robs them of their capacity for reproduction. Throughout my life I have had many great friendships with homosexuals. I've also had great friendships with people who have substance abuse problems. Loving someone does not mean agreeing with everything they do, it just means recognizing the common ground and recognizing the places where your views are relevant and where they're not. You now live in a world where your best friend might not know who his father is and whose mom might be addicted to drugs. You might have another friend who is the only person in his family who speaks English. Another friend might be raised by two moms.

Acknowledging the big picture of deconstruction does not mean condemning or shunning the countless broken byproducts of the carnage. I often think about the many Mexicans I have known personally who are incredible, hardworking and family-oriented people. People I would be honored to call my brothers and sisters. This fact exists simultaneously with the fact that we have a broken immigration system that is by design, deeply destructive to our national fabric. Learn to differentiate between the societal trends people represent and who they actually are as people. Reject the former, embrace the latter. Respect the space and boundaries of your neighbor and treat them with dignity, respect and compassion.

# # #

11

Social Media Batman

Okay private citizen, you've been playing nice at work and been a compassionate friend and neighbor. Now, at last you get to have a bit of fun. The future of discourse lies in the internet and it will prove to be the central battleground for the heart and soul of America. This is where you as private citizen get the opportunity to take the attack to the common enemy: political correctness.

Though I have tremendous respect for the countless conservative crusaders who proudly reveal their names online, if you really want to get aggressive I strongly recommend considering adding a layer of protection between your crusade and your name. It's time to develop an alter ego, someone who can behave far more brashly than your day-job counterpart. Why does Bruce Wayne wear a mask? To protect his family and friends. I recommend developing an online alias for the same reason. Bruce Wayne doesn't save Gotham because he wants recognition, he defends Gotham because it's the right thing to do. It's not about Bruce Wayne, it's about Batman. Find your inner Batman.

One thing that you will quickly discover when you enter the cyber arena is that while we may be outnumbered, our passion as patriots far exceeds that of the countless PC sheeple we will encounter. We are the 300 Spartans making our stand against the degenerate horde. We have spent our entire lives sharpening our ideas against a culture that fought them with denial and suppression. Consequently, we face off against foot soldiers who have spent their entire lives protected from our ideas. As such, we are sufficiently more "combat ready."

When you see a conservative, reach out your cyber hand. Facebook-Friend first; get to know, second. Accordingly, when a fellow conservative crusader posts something, you should 'Like' it first, read it second; and if you have meaningful feedback, respond to it last. By banding with other conservatives, forming cyber wolf packs and getting each other's back, it becomes easier to make bold assertions. You will quickly discover that liberals will quickly retreat when their personal attacks are exposed as meaningless to the discussion. That is not to say that our enemy is feeble or easily defeated. Because most of the young adults running companies like Facebook and Google received thorough brainwashing at their respective universities, our enemies have many inherent advantages in this new arena. They are the gate-keepers of the flow of information, and have free rein to censor or "flag" conservatives for "hateful" content. It's the perfect analogy for the entire Left-Right conversation. Our strength lies in the battle, the actual debate; their strength lies in controlling the board and manipulating the rules. Their success is rooted in preventing conversation; ours rooted in forcing it.

Navigating the Left's privilege as the "admins" of the internet is tricky but not altogether impossible. To avoid flagging I have identified two distinct strategies that seem to work well. One approach involves first recognizing and accepting that there is a hard double standard on the internet. Speech codes are deliberately written vaguely so as to enable their selective application against conservatives. There are countless "F-bomb"-laden Facebook pages advocating violence against white men that somehow avoid the sharp eye of their "community standards" police. Meanwhile you jokingly call your best friend a "fag" for posting a shirtless selfie and you wake up to find your own page frozen or deleted. The hyper disciplined, righteous cyber warrior insists on a high-minded conversation, avoids colorful and controversial language, opting instead to hit his/her enemy with hard, empirical facts. The righteous warrior so severely outclasses his opponents that he gladly takes them on in any arena and by any set of rules they choose before proceeding to completely skewer them using their chosen weapons. Leftists will always try to turn any discussion personal because they generally aren't equipped for an actual debate. The righteous warrior seizes upon these personal attacks and reveals his opponents for the weak-minded cowards they are.

The righteous warrior is a trained assassin, toying with his prey, baiting them along through their pathetic and predictable attack patterns. The actions taken by the righteous warrior are efficient and deliberate and generally void of flair, save the occasionally dry, Bond-esque one-liner. If you hold true to this approach there really isn't much that anyone can do to silence you. Examples of righteous warriors include Ben Shapiro, Dinesh D'Souza and Ann Coulter.

The second approach is that of the berserker. The berserker behaves in a wild and unpredictable manner that might cause you to mistake him/her for an utter lunatic. Unlike the righteous warrior who gets around the admins by playing by their rules, the berserker bombards them with so much objectionable content they become dazed and confused. The berserker appeals to the ideal of a "free internet" that many of the gate-keepers have a soft spot for. He is like a tornado attacking in seemingly random and asymmetric patterns. This cloaks a pointed attack aimed squarely at the various absurdities posed by political correctness. The berserker makes endless sport of things like Rachel Dolezal and soccer helmets for kids. He mockingly applies the principles of deconstruction to deconstruction itself. When the Cultural Marxists call his words offensive he responds by feigning offense at their assumption that his letters were intended to form words. Where the righteous warrior kills by blade the victims of the berserker suffer from internal combustion. Here's an example of how a berserker might make his/her opponent's head explode:

> Liberal: *Wow, another case of racist cops victimizing African-Americans. Good work America.*

Berserker: *Wow, that's pretty offensive that you would assign an ethnicity to the criminals. Or did I miss the part where they mentioned which race they identified with?*

The berserker's use of comedy and his tactic of revealing the absurdity of political correctness by mirroring it paints the liberals into a corner. If we're expected to applaud Caitlyn Jenner's "choice" of gender why do we not extend the same courtesy to Rachel Dolezal? This mocking of political correctness is perhaps the single most important thing that you as a private citizen can do on social media. Twitter is not an ideal forum for a wonky policy discussion; but it's tailor made for terse, snide put-downs. If Facebook is the realm of the righteous warrior, Twitter is the stomping ground of the berserker. Censorship is also virtually non-existent on Twitter, giving the berserker free reign to endlessly mock political correctness. To see a master berserker at work check out the Twitter account of Gavin Macinnes.

# # #

12

Attacking Political Correctness as Media Creator

If it's nothing else, political correctness is absurd. While young hipsters think Stephen Colbert mocking conservatives is hip or cutting edge, it is quite the opposite. It is a strawman rejection of a world that hasn't existed for fifty years. The image of American authority being that of a mean-spirited gym teacher with a military haircut is severely outdated. Today's authority figure is a woman standing before a class of wide-eyed youths reducing all of human history to a naked act of aggression against women. Children have always rebelled against their parents. Today we have the bizarre scenario where young adults, their parents, and their professors all hold the same views as Colbert. If that's not emblematic of a concerted fascist effort to control how Americans think, I don't know what is. The great irony here is that all of these twits, the young hipsters, their parents, their professors and Colbert himself, all believe that they represent a hip counter-culture. Nothing could be further from the truth.

They need to be shaken out of this trance and with just a little bitch-slap we can help bring them back to reality. Once word gets out that the emperor has no clothes... once people begin to see political correctness as ridiculous, it will ultimately prove impossible to put the genie back in the bottle. There will be initial resistance from the leftist dominated entertainment industry to any product that rejects politically correct orthodoxy. Nevertheless, we must endeavor to break through that wall. The common theme here is that our struggle is not necessarily to win points but to have our points heard. Once anti-PC media starts to go viral, once it makes its way to the marketplace, the repudiation of political correctness will catch fire. This will occur for two reasons: it will be edgy and controversial and because it will be undeniably true. Guys like Fox News's Greg Gutfeld have tapped into the wealth of comedic material that comes from political correctness, but we have only scratched the surface. Creating this anti-PC media will not only be an act of public service, I predict that its pioneers will eventually prosper by it. History is full of fortunes made by creative people who identified a vacuum and filled it. There is no greater vacuum than the one that exists in the entertainment industry for humorous content that lampoons politically correct absurdity.

Video activism has proven to be wildly effective. It singlehandedly brought down the Acorn racket and as I sit here writing it may very well be doing the same thing to Planned Parenthood. Andrew Breitbart's "Righteous: Indignation" devotes a good portion of the book to video activism and I highly recommend it to anyone interested in trying their hand at it. The core concepts of a successful video activism campaign involve first identifying a shocking display of Cultural Marxism and then catching it red-handed. Academia is an area ripe for the picking. All across the country the Left has rolled out a deeply graphic and disturbing sex-ed curriculum starting in grade school that promotes all sorts of deviant sexual behaviors to children. Trying to explain what is happening to everyday voters is hard to do as a conservative, due to all the attacks you and your ideas will receive. Let the American people hear the Left tell in their own words precisely what their ideas are regarding, for example, gender and sexuality, and things will take care of themselves.

There are laws in place that prevent people from being recorded without their consent. One way to approach this is by baiting your enemies into public areas like restaurants, as the anti-Planned Parenthood activists have done. Another is to simply hide your motives, present yourself as a fellow do-good Cultural Marxist and ask your enemies to present their views with pride and have them sign off on the recording. Most of these assholes are so thoroughly indoctrinated in their perverse worldview that they have no idea that their views are even controversial. Breitbart lays out a concrete blueprint for releasing your videos to the media. It relies on anticipating their predictable actions and using it to your advantage. Get videos from different parts of the country, then start by releasing the videos from only one of these areas. The first defense of the enemy will come from an expectation that the events were isolated. Wait for them to make this claim, then promptly prove them wrong. They'll say your tapes are heavily edited. Leave the best parts out of your first cut. Again, their patterns are fairly one-dimensional, and once you get the hang of how the media elites operate you will find predicting their actions relatively simple.

That doesn't mean it will be easy. Where our enemy is dim-witted and slow she is also big and strong... and wields enormous influence. If you decide to attack them using video activism you *will* be attacked personally. You *will* be subjected to violent character assassination and you and your family *will* likely receive threats of violence. You may also suffer legal attacks, lawsuits etc. The video activist is a brave warrior, far braver than I. Frankly, I can only recommend it for those that don't have much to lose. Young adults, college students, people who haven't started out yet. For brave young adults video activism can lead to a career platform. For established professionals it can lead to the destruction and loss of everything you've worked for. Proceed with caution video activists—we salute your service to the country.

A remarkable event occurred several years ago that you likely never got to hear. It's the story of a man named Thomas Ball who committed suicide by setting himself on fire on the steps of a New Hampshire court house to protest the very real "war on men." He wrote a lengthy and detailed suicide note chronicling how the Family Court system denied him due process, criminalized him and reduced him to effective slavery. More profoundly, it documents with empirical evidence how men all across the country are subjected to this same injustice.

His work is well-researched, profound and compelling. I encourage anyone reading this to find it online. How is it that a story so horrific—of a man actually setting himself on fire on the steps of a court house—is completely suppressed? First and foremost, the mainstream media quickly and efficiently filtered the story out of rotation because there was no possible way to deconstruct it into their narrative. Unfortunately, Fox News didn't give the story any play either, at least that I'm aware of. The dominance of political correctness is so pervasive that much of conservatism is co concerned with being punished for offending PC sensibilities that they too are afraid of powerful stories.

Thomas Ball should be regarded as a martyr, if not a national hero. Unfortunately though, he gave the media the tools they needed to silence his story. Included in his thorough researching and harsh indictment of the legal assault perpetrated against fathers by the judicial system was a call for violence. This provided the perfect excuse for the MSM to avoid the story. He was attempting to actually incite real revolution, so therefore it became dangerous to present it to the public. It also enabled them to dismiss the majority of his factual grievances as the rantings of a violent, domestic terrorist.

The moral of the story is clear. The power of the enemy to silence you is massive; don't make it easy on them. Had Ball done a better job strategizing his protest it might have made more of an impact. Powerful content alone can prove meaningless without an accompanying plan for serving it up to the masses. Nevertheless, this book honors his service and I encourage everyone to become versed in his story and to spread it.

# # #

13

Battling Political Correctness as a Politician

When we discuss preparing our conservative politicians to effectively combat political correctness the first step is to slap the stupid out of (most of) them. Most notably, the preposterous notion that we must surrender on social issues in order to remain relevant. The fact that this strategy is so popular speaks to the degree that the Left has mind-fucked the Republican Party. The behavior is similar to that of a mouse that has been so severely savaged by a cat that its dizziness leads it to return to the cat.

I refer to conservatives that suffer from this dementia as "McAvoy" Republicans—the inspiration curtesy of Aaron Sorkin's hilarious HBO drama, *The Newsroom*. For people not familiar with his work it is the height of what I call "lib camp": political drama written by liberals that is so obnoxiously pretentious and arrogant that it becomes laughable. The star of *Newsroom* is Will McAvoy (played by Jeff Daniels), a presumed "responsible" Republican newscaster who is appalled by the rise of the alleged extreme right and begrudgingly goes about calling them out on their craziness. Will McAvoy is the poster boy for the type of Republicans that are "permissible" to the Left. The type that avoids those dastardly and divisive social issues so that they can focus on the things that really matter, like changing our marginal tax rates by 1 or 2 points. The other term that has emerged for this dementia is "cuckservativism," a play on "cuckold." A cuckservative watches his country get screwed while he smiles and pays for the bill, balances the finances etc. You're welcome to use these two terms interchangeably but for the sake of this book I'll use the term I coined.

We are facing a strain of communism that adapted from the failed, original virus that focused primarily on class warfare. Political correctness and Cultural Marxism theorize that the most successful way to spread communism is to focus first on deconstructing a people's cultural and social mores. Any conservative who supports the "clever" strategy of combatting liberalism by surrendering on social issues is a moron. This is the equivalent of responding to a naval assault by calling for the cavalry. When you are being attacked, as America is by the Cultural Marxists, you do not have the luxury of choosing the battleground. If you can't understand such a simple concept you have no business in the political arena. The strategy is doubly flawed because it assumes that a surrender on social issues would put an end to the Culture War. The Left will never stop deconstructing our culture until there is nothing left of it but an amorphous amalgam of moral relativism. If conservatives stand down on social issues all it will do is embolden the Left and increase the rate at which they deconstruct our culture.

McAvoy Republicans are not only ineffectual, they frequently act as saboteurs. We have a horrible habit as a movement of parroting the various lies of the Left. Speaking of clever ideas, whoever trademarked the idea of accusing Democrats of waging the "real" war on women should have their speaking privileges permanently revoked. Conservatives should only address the phony "war on women" to soundly debunk it before pivoting to the very real *war on men.*

The Left has convinced much of the country that up is down, right is wrong and black is white. Conservatism will continue to lose so long as the politically correct paradigm reigns supreme. When political correctness has successfully forced both parties to kneel before its alter the Cultural Marxists will take their victory lap. At that point, whether the sitting president is Democrat or Republican is irrelevant as the values of the country will already have been completely wiped away.

This is not to say that candidates cannot be pragmatic in certain areas of the country. I don't begrudge a blue-state Republican from making tactical decisions to focus on issues he or she thinks they can win with—provided they have been properly educated on political correctness and don't betray the greater cause of resisting it. I don't just advocate social conservatism for the big picture, I also firmly believe that more often than not it proves helpful in winning individual campaigns. I have long maintained that social issues are the true Achilles heel of the Democratic Party, particularly with their minority constituents. It's one of the reasons they react so violently whenever they are challenged on them. When we make the mistake of avoiding social issues we give the Democrats a pass on explaining their true vision of the world to the electorate. This is a huge mistake. We must constantly force our enemies to explain the intended and unintended outcomes that will spring from every societal experimentation they champion.

The great irony about the Left's coalition of African-Americans and third world minorities is that those cultures place tremendous importance upon both faith and family. The decadence required to contemplate "gender theory" is one afforded only to the affluent. Struggling, lower-income communities regard faith and family more as necessities for survival than as items of fashion. Go to the black churches in Alabama and ask them their thoughts on gender-neutral restrooms. Because Obama had home court advantage with minorities, he was able to get away with pushing a radical social agenda while simultaneously commanding the votes of groups that find many of his ideas intrinsically repugnant.

It remains to be seen how these communities will respond to being lectured on social issues by a wealthy white woman such as Hillary Clinton. If applied correctly the Left's overreach on social issues could once again prove to be their undoing as it was in 2004. George W. Bush managed to win re-election in the midst of an unpopular, crumbling war by standing up in defense of marriage. Admittedly, that was over ten years ago and the Left has advanced the country considerably further in their direction since then. Nevertheless, I believe a majority coalition can once again be forged by appealing to the working people of all ethnicities that hold traditional values consistent with universal sound natural principles.

We will never be able to make inroads within these minority groups by mimicking the Democrats. We must stop playing the identity politics game. Trying to beat your enemy at a game they created and mastered is a fool's errand. We don't need Hispanic-Republican clubs nor do we need clubs for any other of the groups bestowed with victim status by the Left. We are not the party that divides everyone into groups and plays them against one another. We are the party that believes as Martin Luther King did that the measure of a person lies in the content of his or her character. We welcome people of all ethnicities to take part in America. Our selling point is the improved standard of living and the empowerment that comes with realizing one's own potential. In a conversation about values, ours have the distinct advantage of being grounded in reality and of having a proven track record of success. Don't assume that minorities cannot grasp these concepts. Have faith that they will. The various ways a person can be categorized are really quite insignificant. Trust in the message and trust in the hearts of men.

The Left has broken the country into pieces. We are no longer a country of common purpose and ambition—let alone ancestry. The key to forming a lasting coalition that can get America back on course lies in discovering things that unite us all. For a movement started by communists, Cultural Marxism ironically holds a hidden contempt for the common working man. We must seek out the common men and women of the country, be they white or brown, and stand with them. The handful of elites that dictate the liberal agenda have very little in common with these people and this will become blatantly obvious with a properly framed national discussion.

One thing the Left is good at is using strawman arguments to defeat conservatives. This is a luxury afforded to them by their monopoly over public discourse. It therefore becomes important for us to reflect on our arguments and scrap the ones consistently dismantled by our opponents. The Left's general goal in a debate will be to reduce us to Bible-thumping, gun-toting southern redneck caricatures of conservatives. If you want to see how big a liberal's eyes can get quote a

Biblical passage to make an argument. They will pounce on you so fast your head will spin. This is not to suggest abandoning your faith; quite the opposite. The problem is that we are using religious freedom as a debate crutch at the expense of learning the more effective techniques that employ rationalism. If you really delve deep into the beliefs of Cultural Marxists it ultimately speaks to a godless reality where man alone is responsible for his destiny. God will sort them out eventually but our government is man-made and because we have a separation of church and state we must predicate our arguments on truths that everyone accepts. If the people you are debating with don't share your understanding of God, how can you expect them to take Him by his word? Stick to hard, empirical facts. Many social issues regarded as religious ones, like marriage and abortion, have far more compelling arguments that are derived from Natural Law. Liberals claim to have reverence for science and reason, so try challenging them to explain their reproductive views, for example within the framework of biology.

Because the Left is always pushing into new frontiers of insanity there will always be an opportunity to fight them on social issues. As mentioned earlier, the key is to bring the fight to them before they have the chance to frame the debate for the public. Now that they've successfully normalized homosexuality their next objective is to slide down from LGB to T for transgenderism. The Republican platform should include an insistence that transgenderism be regarded as a mental illness. Arguing that a man who wants to remove his penis suffers from delusion is a pretty easy argument to win. And yet in the court of public opinion, we're already losing that debate. Be proactive not reactive.

Adopt a populist, economic platform focusing on the middle class. We need to stake out our claim as the party of the blue-collar working American. If we must make concessions to the Left, here is the place to do so. If you are backed into a corner and must concede ground to the enemy give them the ground that can be easily recovered. For instance, all that is needed to correct our bloated tax code is to pass a new one. Contrast that with policies that pertain to our national fabric. It took the Left decades to alter the demographics of the country. It took them decades to change us from a country where intact households were the norm to one where fragmented, single-parent homes are practically the majority. At the end of the day, the systematic dismantling of the mother and father household proves to be the most devastating crime perpetrated against the American people. There is no magical switch to flip; no law to pass that restores the primacy of the biological nuclear family. Political correctness is a virus, and right now our immune system has proven incapable of combatting it. Our enemies began by emphasizing economic Marxism first. It didn't get them very far. They evolved to a far more successful movement by putting the primary focus on Cultural Marxism. We've spent fifty years focusing on economic conservatism first. It hasn't worked. If we have any hope of surviving we, too must adapt and evolve.

We're not just here because we've lost elections. We've actually won a great deal of elections along the way. Therefore it follows that our problem is not just winning elections but also governing effectively once in power. Part of the reason why proper education on political correctness is so important is because so many of its tentacles are hidden from plain sight. As such, at this very moment countless simplistic Republican politicians preside over the forces of evil without any inkling of knowledge about it. Republicans must learn to identify policies and programs rooted in Cultural Marxism and swiftly amputate them. Obama famously advocated the use of a scalpel over a machete when speaking about the economy. It was a great line and it's true, the Left has been using a scalpel for quite some time. The issue is that they have been using the scalpel to carefully cut the country apart rather than tactfully cutting back on its spending and encroachment on liberty and freedom.

One area where political correctness is not hard to spot is academia. In the ideological war for America academia represents the front line of the battle—and I don't think we even have any boots on the ground. There are a handful of books written that talk about the catastrophe, but to my knowledge the Republican Party has done very little to put out the fire. I don't even think many of them know it's there. What Scott Walker did to the teachers' unions in Wisconsin is a blueprint for what needs to be done all across the country. Why do you think he received death threats, threats against his wife and children? When you go for the heart of the beast you see its true ugliness. In spite of all that, what he did was just the start of what is needed.

The entire educational system has become so infested with the cancer of political correctness that you almost have to start from complete scratch. Everything from the selection of literature to the courses and the professors and faculty themselves, reek with the stench of political correctness. At this very moment our children are being "educated" by people that are effectively cultural terrorists. In a saner time any adult caught distributing our current sex-ed curriculum to children would be prosecuted for child abuse. The first step to restoring America lies in enacting a massive restraining order between American children and the perverts that comprise the academic elite. I'm fully supportive of building a wall between the United States and Mexico—after the wall is built between Cultural Marxism and public education. Political correctness should not be allowed within fifty yards of a school zone, and until the current deviants calling the shots are removed any federal dollar spent in education is money spent harming our children and our country.

Political correctness must be removed both root and branch. You must scour your state's various taxpayer funded initiatives. Anything with social justice code words like "tolerance" or "diversity" must be defunded. We must also pull the plug on any and all groups, organizations or foundations designed to serve any specific gender or ethnic groups. We've just begun to combat the false charges of bigotry leveled against us by the Left. We must go beyond repudiating this slander. We must go on the attack. We must expose and label the Democratic Party as the agents of anti-white, anti-male, anti-Christian hatred. Reaching out to minority groups is important, yes—but I would argue that when you're facing a party whose entire coalition is galvanized around the demonization of white men and yet you only receive 72% of the white male vote, you are underperforming. There is absolutely no reason why any white man should ever vote for a Democrat. Start by securing all of the votes from the groups being antagonized by the Left first before expanding into the groups whose votes they are currently buying. The first comes naturally, the second requires patience and care.

In a different age I might have been a libertarian. "Live and let live" sounds really nice to me but unfortunately this is no time for neutrality. America has been broken, even more so than is visibly apparent today. When you look at the country today you have to realize that half of it was raised in a time before the Cultural Marxists called the shots. But that generation is fading into the sunset and eventually the sun will set on their values, too. Values that were tested by time, values that they got from their parents and so on and so forth. Ready to replace them is the second, third and fourth waves of politically correct America. It's not sufficient to merely stop the bleeding to save the country at this point in time. We've lost too much. Republican leadership must actually set to work rebuilding and restoring the American family and its values. It is not enough to put an end to the incentivizing of negative behavior, we must give positive reinforcement to people engaged in life-affirming behavior. We must endeavor to reconstruct our deconstructed culture.

The Culture War matters because when we stop at the grocery store to spend the money we've earned after working an eleven-hour day we like being served by people that know how to put on pants, count change and speak English. Because when we come home with this week's groceries we like smelling last week's in the oven. Because when we unwind before bed we like being able to turn on the television without seeing our values and way of life continually mocked. Because when our families go out to dinner on special occasions we like being able to dine in peace without being subjected to loud, degrading music. Because we like being able to put our children in the care of public schools without worrying about what perverted propaganda they will be subjected to. I question any conservative who views these issues as secondary to things like the economy and national security. Not because those issues don't matter—they matter greatly—but because these issues can only matter within the context of a free and dignified society. If we surrender our culture what then does it matter what the dollar buys and what our troops are defending?

# # #

14

Conclusion

What is a nation? Is it a group of people with common ethnic backgrounds? Is it defined by its borders? Is it their language, their culture? Is it their religion, their beliefs and their ideals? Whatever a nation is, political correctness wants America to be the opposite.

We have defined political correctness, touched on its history and its rise to power in America. We have also examined some of its chief weapons and sought out its weaknesses.

The inescapable conclusion is that we are living in the age of political correctness and that we are surrounded by its evil. The repugnant stench of Cultural Marxism permeates and pollutes virtually every aspect of American life. It breathes through your radio, it dances on your television. It not only controls your president and his party but to a large degree it controls the Republican Party as well. The Republicans have been so severely traumatized by the whippings that even the staunchest of conservatives thinks twice before defending anything that might offend politically correct orthodoxy.

Political correctness has ravaged your family, subjected countless people to the agony of social chaos and confusion. It has done all this while arrogantly claiming a moral high ground. From the day we step foot in kindergarten we are taught to follow the teachings of political correctness as if it were the national religion. This is because political correctness aimed to kill our God and take His place. To an outsider it might look as though it has succeeded. We know better than that. Our God is eternal; our God is present in the room when life is conceived. When the half that is man is made whole by the holy union with woman we partake in His eternal nature. Political correctness is a god of death and the inevitable path of those that follow it will subsequently prove to be death. We needn't worry about our God, his glory is eternal and in the morning it will shine. Let your heart be contented by this fact, but if it must worry let it worry for those being marched into the fire. You and your family will forever be safe in the heart of your creator.

# # #

Epilogue

By 2008 America had descended into social chaos. A thoroughly broken immigration system had led to a massive shift in the country's demographics. Our greatest strength as a society, the intact mother-father household, had been relegated from the ideal standard to merely one of many (and often times bizarre or perverse) configurations.

Two generations of educated adults had been funneled through indoctrination camps masquerading as educational institutions. Americans as a whole were generally disoriented, broken and largely dysfunctional. The younger half of the country had fully embraced a radically anti-American worldview informed by the values of political correctness. In other words, the country had become everything the secular progressives had dreamed it could be—and more.

On top of all this, the country had just sat through eight years of a failed Republican presidency that crescendoed with a massive economic collapse. The individuals represented by these disturbing social trend lines would come to be known as the Obama coalition, and they would easily carry him to victory in not only 2008 but 2012 as well. But it was a victory secured decades earlier by the party which would come to worship him as their figurehead.

During the 50's, 60's and 70's the Democratic Party cleverly snatched up all the figurative stock on non-traditional, particularly non-white Americans. After securing these various demographical and behavior-based groups, they then set out to grow them from proverbial "penny stocks" into substantial voting blocks, whilst simultaneously devaluing the stock of the white, Judeo-Christian peoples once known simply as Americans.

Affirmative Action policies, originally designed to specifically address the unique and real plight of African-Americans, evolved into a blank handout check for anyone not white or male. Immigration policies and attitudes were reorganized away from prioritizing assimilation and productivity, instead placing value on immigrants who increased "diversity." Our national history and moral identity was cast aside and we embraced the concept of multiculturalism as the singularly supreme purpose of our country. The god of multiculturalism condemned the audacity of our achievements and commanded us to endlessly repent in hopes of someday atoning for our inherent white guilt. It would inform us to actively encourage the celebration and recognition of any and all ethnic or cultural identities save those of white Europeans.

White European cultural pride received an exclusive, lifetime ban from our new diversity-centric society, and anyone who pushed back on these rules was swiftly branded a white supremacist. The freedom to openly celebrate cultural identity became the first of many privileges granted to the Left's newly founded protected victim groups in exchange for political support. This would prove to be just the beginning of what would become a fifty-plus-year campaign to demonize and marginalize whites in their own communities.

Ironically for the do-good white voters who supported Obama out of the unspoken promise that he would forever pardon them of their white guilt, he would proceed to do just the opposite. Anyone that voted for Obama in hopes of a "post-racial" America was proven to be wildly naive. He did not offer up his presidency to

Americans of all colors as irrefutable proof that we had overcome the racial tension of our past. Instead, Obama and his race-crazed cabinet of militant, black power thugs like Eric Holder would end up driving race relations back into the 50s and 60s.

Rather than attempting to address alarming trends from the African-American community he called home, he and his politically charged DOJ shamelessly cited their appalling violent crime rates as an excuse to finger and frisk law enforcement over phantom racial biases. By routinely siding with criminals in high profile altercations that demanded police intervention, he helped foster a climate of hostility and distrust towards law enforcement that led to the murder of several police officers. He also routinely covered for Muslim extremists in the wake of horrific terrorist attacks; and the administration was often caught red-handed attempting to conceal blatant religious motivations from the public.

When pushed on these issues he responded with disgust, routinely lecturing Christians and shifting the conversation to gun control. In the Middle East he intervened against a strong, incumbent prime minister of our historical ally Israel whilst simultaneously attempting to cozy up with Iran, a nation that routinely calls for their and our destruction.

Obama's legacy and actions are hard to fathom when viewed through the prism of a president attempting to advance American interests at home and abroad. Only when we view his presidency through the lens of a man attempting to undermine, disrupt and dismantle our way of life, does it begin to make sense.

Clearly, Obama's strategy was to utilize the bully pulpit like a crow bar, jam it into our national fabric and expand the various demographic, behavioral and ideological trends that led to his election. He and his party's singular focus is to poke holes into America until she is impossible to keep afloat and we are forced to abandon ship and accept a life trapped in the life jackets of socialism.

Over time, as the demographics continued to shift in favor of the Democrats, it would become increasingly difficult, if not impossible, for a Republican (at least what we currently understand a Republican to be) to ever reclaim the White House. The Left was so committed to this strategy that they accepted the idea of a permanently Republican Congress as a necessary and acceptable loss in order to push forward on their long game. Obama and his party sat back and watched as Republicans regained the Senate as well as a near 2-to-1 advantage in governorships without ever entertaining a course correction. Just the opposite, weeks after losing a mid-term wave election centered largely on immigration, he doubled down on the topic and openly defied the American people by unilaterally issuing an executive order granting amnesty to millions of illegals. Ultimately they theorized that those other branches of government, like the white working class voters that placed them into power, would prove to be irrelevant.

Presidents appoint Supreme Court Justices as well as the judgeships in lower federal courts that feed into it, and a permanently Democratic executive branch would in time lead to a permanently liberal judicial branch as well. They would then use these two branches to govern the American people like a vice grip, issuing increasingly dictatorial Executive Orders that would all inevitably be rubber-stamped by a radically progressive Supreme Court. In this scenario, individuals, states and even Congress are at the mercy of tyrannical presidents and the activist judges they appoint.

The Democratic Party abandoned Middle America and their blue-collar base in favor of national identity politics and the third-world peasants they recruited to vote them out of existence. They took a calculated risk that the influx of new voters hungry for big-government largesse that flooded into the electorate as a result of their policies would offset the inevitable "white flight" out of their coalition.

Because Obama did such a masterful job of puncturing the dam, perpetuating social chaos and galvanizing minorities against whites, he can't be blamed for their recent defeat. The failure came in his party's severe miscalculation in ignoring all of the red flags and insisting on trying to ram Hillary Clinton down the throats of an electorate that simply did not like her, for a host of reasons. Lost in the media's obsession with demonstrating how the 58% of white Americans who supported Trump were doing so entirely out of racism, was the fact that race might have had something to do with the 90+% support Obama enjoyed from the African-American community. You see, it turns out that brown people just don't vote with the same enthusiasm for a privileged white woman lecturing them on social issues as they would for Barack Obama.

As I predicted in 2014, Hillary was caught in the unenviable position of attempting to pick up new, working-class white voters while simultaneously demonizing them to the urban population centers she sought to keep energized. Ultimately, Clinton was done in by the fact that she failed to offer any new voters to offset the loss of Obama's home court advantage with minorities. In the end the only people who were truly excited about Hillary's candidacy were lesbians and academics, most of whom had already voted twice for Obama.

Had Hillary won, the Left likely would have succeeded in finalizing their end game, but due to an unlikely twist of fate the pendulum now swings in the opposite direction.

Trump was a deeply flawed candidate with a maddening talent for unforced errors. But he was also bold, refreshing, and distinctly American. He provided a clear contrast between not only Democrats but many Republicans, on the issues that mattered most to the American people. These weren't the typical identity politics-based issues that the media consistently told us would define the election. These were real, meat-and-potatoes issues like immigration, jobs and law and order.

Ironically, after decades of crying wolf about the sexism, racism and homophobia of Mormon boy scouts like Mitt Romney or esteemed POWs like John McCain, the media finally got the real deal with Trump. But they had already squandered their credibility, and their standard shenanigans ultimately fell flat on independent voters who broke heavily for Trump.

Earlier in the year I wrote that whichever party won this election would be in a strong position to bury their opponent for a solid decade or two. If Hillary won it would be because the gravity of the entitlement class would prove too large to prevent the country from sinking into socialism. If however, she managed to lose, so much of what the Left has accomplished collapses like a house of cards. Despite being the dominant party of the past decade, the Democratic Party's power base has grown incredibly hollow and their intellectual vigor has largely atrophied from lack of use. They preside over a laughably narrow and largely irrelevant platform consisting of nonsense like transgender bathrooms and "sanctuary cities." Ideas that require the continual hectoring, lecturing and shaming of Americans to force them into submission—but what figures of authority does the Democratic Party have left to pull this off?

There is no bench of rising stars eager to lead them into the future because an entire generation of would-be Democratic leaders had their careers aborted prematurely during the two mid-term massacres. Republicans now have twice as many Governors as well as majorities in both the House and the Senate. Now that conservatives have the crowning jewel of a Republican president, the party is the strongest it has been in nearly a century.

Sure, the Left still controls academia, and late-night television is still littered with talentless SJWs, but the seats had already started emptying before Trump's election. It will also prove more difficult to politicize their classrooms and TV programs so heavily without having a president routinely calling into their award ceremonies congratulating them on their virtue-signaling.

Beyond representation in the government, conservative dominance exists on all levels from grassroots organization all the way down to the average American citizen so disgusted by the omnipresent political correctness that they are but one insult away from active involvement in the political process. Leftists have relied so long on their ability to censor opposing views rather than confronting them that most have lost the ability to debate conservatives with any level of maturity. Meanwhile, after decades of suppression and ridicule, everyday conservatives are fundamentally sharper if for no other reason than they've been forced to become so. The Left's entire playbook was built around their ability to play with a lead, and now it remains to be seen how effective they will be at playing from behind, as they most certainly will be for the next four years.

A few months ago it looked like Scalia's replacement would be selected by Hillary Clinton or Barack Obama. Today we know that Donald Trump will be the one replacing not only him but likely at least one of the three left-leaning justices north of seventy-eight. Furthermore, because the vast majority of Obama's "accomplishments" were achieved without consensus and by circumventing Congress, they are largely reversible with the stroke of a pen.

The Democrats were dealt a strong hand and a favorable flop. They went for the kill; they were "all in." Sometimes in life as in poker, luck beats strategy. It all looked good for the Democrats going into the final card but somehow, perhaps by the grace of God, America was bailed out "on the river." For eight long years the secular progressives looked down contemptuously upon a working class of Americans who were largely powerless to intervene as they inflicted their various sociological experiments upon the country. In a supremely fitting twist of poetic justice these very same elites will now be forced to sit back and watch in sheer horror as we MAKE AMERICA GREAT AGAIN.

# # #

About the Author

Daryl Kane is the host of the popular conservative podcast, "Right-Wing Road Trip with Daryl Kane," and editor of the conservative website, "Revenge of the Patriot." Aside from his work as a political pundit, he works as a motivational speaker, fiction writer and film producer.